SEOUL
Like a Local

BY THE PEOPLE WHO CALL IT HOME

SEOUL

Like a Local

BY THE PEOPLE WHO CALL IT HOME

Contents

meet the locals

BETH EUNHEE HONG
A copy editor and podcaster for The Korea Herald, *Korean Canadian Beth spends her free time at comedy open mics or enjoying wine by the Han River.*

ARIAN KHAMENEH
Danish journalist Arian initially moved to Seoul for summer school. He spends his days reporting on stories and his nights at underground clubs.

ALLISON NEEDELS
When she's not studying for her Ph.D. in Korean art history, American-born Allison runs a travel website about her second home.

CHARLES USHER
Now back in the US, Charles spent 12 years in Seoul, teaching English, editing a magazine, and walking the city with his wife and their Jindo mix.

Seoul
WELCOME TO THE CITY

Seoul is many things, but a city stuck in the past it is not. Life moves fast here, so much so that visit more than once and you'll discover a city much-changed – a fresh landmark here, a new cultural hotspot there, that chic little coffee shop you once discovered gone without a trace. Indeed, one of the first expressions you'll hear in Seoul is *ppalli ppalli* ("hurry up"), and unabashedly chasing the new is what drives this city.

Yet, even when Seoul is changing at speed, its people maintain a deep connection to their cultural heritage. Restaurants may try new dishes and undergo sleek facelifts, but you can always guarantee a hearty bowl of kimchi stew, made from a recipe that's been handed down through the generations. The city's expressive youth might fill their wardrobes with branded sneakers and oversized hoodies, but they still find occasion to wear *hanbok* – traditional dress

that's so loved, it has its own dedicated holiday in October. And, sure, K-pop is fresh and exciting, but locals are just as obsessed with centuries-old folk music known as *gugak* (which is, in fact, influencing K-pop tunes more and more these days).

Still, while Seoul does have its constants, it can be hard to find your bearings in a city where so much is happening all the time, and a truly exhaustive guide for such a place may never be possible. This book, rather, is a peek into the pastimes that Seoulites hold dear, like barbecuing meat on a repurposed steel drum, drinking through the night at a *pocha*, and ambling through narrow streets lined with *hanok*. It's these things that make up the city's core identity, and which endure no matter how many cafés close or skyscrapers shoot up. So, *ppalli ppalli* and start exploring – Seoul won't wait.

Liked by the locals

"Seoul is never boring. Even after living here for more than ten years, I'm still fascinated by the endless permutations of old and new, local and global – in the street style, architecture, food, music, and so much more."

BETH EUNHEE HONG, COPY EDITOR

Sport extravaganzas in the spring, alfresco parties in the summer, spa soaks in the winter – there's always something going on in this lively city.

Seoul
THROUGH THE YEAR

SPRING

BALLPARK BLOWOUT
Spring swings into Seoul with the start of the Korean Baseball Organization (KBO) season in April, when fans pack out stadiums to cheer on their favorite teams while waving elaborate props.

FLOWER GAZING
You know it's spring when pretty pastel tones take over every social media feed. Bask in the real-life beauty of cherry blossoms by strolling along Yeouido's riverfront and in Seoul Grand Park.

RIVERSIDE PICNICS
The first warm day of the year means one thing: picnicking along the Han River. It's an extravagant affair, with tents, camping gear, and impressive spreads of food and drink consumed by friends all day long.

SUMMER

FESTIVAL FUN
Seoul's festival calendar is jam-packed year-round, but summer is arguably when festivals are the most jubilant. Some unmissable events include the Sinchon Water Gun Festival, a massive public water gun fight in July, and the Pentaport Rock Festival, a day of local and international music in August.

COOLING DOWN
Summers in Seoul are hot and humid, and wouldn't be survivable without two things: *bingsu*, a shaved iced

dessert, and *naengmyeon*, a cold buckwheat noodle soup. Still can't shake the sweats? Follow the locals to the coast surrounding the Korean peninsula for a dose of cooler air.

MONSOON MOOCHING

August, the hottest stretch of summer, is usually preceded by a bout of monsoons, seasonal rains that fall in late June and July and last for up to two weeks. It's around this time that locals see the latest exhibitions at the city's free museums (thank you, air con).

FALL

LEAF PEEPING

Cherry blossom is *so* last season, with fall ushering in a vivid tapestry of earthy yellows and rich reds. Some stay in Seoul to enjoy the colors, while others day-trip out to tree-lined Nami Island.

HEAVENLY HIKES

Clear skies and cool temperatures provide the perfect conditions for a Seoulite's favorite pastime: hiking. Many mountains surround the city, but the best panoramic view of Seoul comes from the tallest, Bukhansan.

FLYING SPARKS

Seoulites see out the fall with a bang – literally, at the Seoul International Fireworks Festival in October. Friends hit up Banpo Bridge early to secure the best spot from which to watch fireworks dazzle over the Han River.

WINTER

BLISSFUL BATHS

While heavy snowfall is rare, winter in Seoul can still be brutally cold. To warm up, people head to *jjimjilbang* (public bathhouses) to soak in hot baths and clay saunas.

COZY DINING

Dark, cold nights call for one thing: gathering the gang at a BBQ joint. Sitting around hot coals and grilling meat while warming up with shots of soju is as good as it gets.

OUTDOOR ANTICS

Some people choose to hibernate in the winter, but others throw themselves full throttle into the chilly weather, heading out of Seoul to nearby ski resorts for a week – or even just a day – on the slopes.

In a city where fitting in is the norm, it's important to understand the dos and don'ts of daily life, from subway manners to tipping. Here's a starting point.

Seoul
KNOW-HOW

For a directory of health and safety resources, safe spaces and accessibility information, turn to page 186. For everything else, read on.

There's no denying that there are certain customs and traditions within Korea, and describing them all could fill a book in itself. Having said that, most Seoulites are pretty relaxed when it comes to cultural slip-ups. Our advice? Take any online lists of "must-follow" customs lightly, and simply be open-minded when locals request you take part in, and follow, their cultural standards.

EAT
Mealtimes aren't strictly followed in Korea – locals eat at every hour of the day, whether it's at a BBQ house or a street food market. Restaurants tend to open in the morning, and when they close in the late evening, 24-hour convenience stores are a savior, selling snacks like cup ramen that you can cook using the store's microwaves.

A typical meal
Korean meals all have a communal element, mostly in the form of *banchan*: side dishes, often including seasoned vegetables, that are made to share. So strong is the communal dining experience in Korea that eating alone was long considered taboo. While this culture is shifting, with many restaurants now providing tables for soloists, most menus offer large meals to split between 3 to 6 people.

Korea has a love affair with meat, so if you're vegan or vegetarian, it's best to find a plant-based-friendly restaurant or speak to your server before ordering. The same goes for allergies: seafood, for one, is often present in Korean food, even if it's not immediately apparent.

Table manners

Good table manners go a long way in Seoul. Closest to the chopsticks? It's polite to distribute them around the table. No one will berate you for not knowing how to use chopsticks, but they will be offended if you stick them vertically in the middle of the rice bowl – a gesture used for rites honoring the dead. It's also rude to poke around in shared dishes with chopsticks. Not so rude? Slurping, so go right ahead.

DRINK

Seoul's drinking scene is mostly talked about in relation to coffee or alcohol. Let's start with coffee. Seoul famously has more coffee shops per capita than Seattle – so much so that certain areas are home to so-called "café streets," entire roads dedicated to coffee shops.

Alcohol consumption, meanwhile, can come as a shock to visitors; Korea has the highest rates of alcohol drinking in Asia. Alcohol is commonly seen as a social necessity, which can come with a pressure to drink. If you don't feel up for drinking, inform your host; they may ask a few more times following your rejection, but Seoul has gotten much better at respecting abstinence. Alcohol is also rarely enjoyed without small plates of food known as *anju*, with favorites being dried squid or seafood pancakes.

Keep in mind

Here are some more tips and tidbits that will help you fit in like a local.

» **Card is king** Nearly everywhere accepts credit cards. If you see a local using cash, it probably means they've lost their card.

» **Don't tip** Tipping isn't required, and can be offensive – if you tip, you may have a surprised Korean chasing after you to return it.

» **No smoking** Smoking is banned indoors, at outdoor areas of cafés, and near metro or bus stations. To light up, find a smoking area.

» **Shoes off** Koreans never wear shoes in the home, or in most older restaurants.

Drinking rules

Much like with eating, there are certain table manners to keep in mind when drinking. A key one? It's always polite to pour drinks for others, and to make sure their cup is never empty. They'll do the same for you, and that's a ritual worthy of a *geonbae* (cheers).

SHOP

While many countries in Asia are known for their haggling culture at markets, it's not as big a thing here. Nonetheless, big purchases are more likely to get you a discount, and paying with cash will win you favors (yes, cash does have its place here sometimes). Given how late people work, most stores, malls, and markets are open daily from 10am to 10pm, satiating a love for shopping.

ARTS & CULTURE

While all national museums in Korea are free, private institutions aren't; it's worth pre-booking your visits to these. Places can get very crowded on the weekends, too, so visit in the week if you can. Pay attention to "no photography" signs, especially when visiting temples. And, on that note, remember that temples are places of worship for locals: show respect, maintain a respectful silence, and wear loose clothing that covers most of your body.

NIGHTLIFE

Seoulites work famously long hours, so nights out are a release – and can be a marathon. You might hear talk of 1-*cha*, 2-*cha*, 3-*cha*, and so on – *cha* simply means rounds, or stops, on a night out. A typical 1-*cha* (round one) involves a meal, likely at a BBQ place or a *pocha* (tent restaurant). It's then on to a club or bar, followed by a session at a *noraebang* (singing room). Missed the last train at 2am? It's common to stay out until the subway gets going again at 5:30am.

Most clubs near universities don't require an ID, but upscale areas such as Gangnam, Itaewon, and Jongno will often card visitors. Oh, and when deciding what to wear, err on the side of dressing up, rather than down.

OUTDOORS

Half of Korea's population lives in Seoul, so streets, parks, and hiking trails can get busy. Make room for people to pass at crowded points on trails and stay out of bike lines. Enjoying a picnic? Waste baskets are everywhere, so clean up after yourself, please.

LGBTQ+ SCENE

The emergence of LGBTQ+ rights in Korea has been slow, and same-sex marriage is not recognized. However, rights and attitudes within society are changing, and the Seoul Queer Culture Festival has taken place since 2000.

Though small, Seoul's queer scene is thriving, with everything from shops to bars run by the LGBTQ+ community. For safety reasons, many places don't explicitly state their queer background, and get most patrons via word of mouth; those included in this book *(p154)* openly identify as queer spaces on social media at the time of writing. If you feel uneasy at any point, consult the resources listed on page 186.

LANGUAGE

The Korean alphabet is relatively easy to learn, with only 24 letters. Romanized versions of Korean, which appear on the likes of menus and street signs, are a life-saver for visitors, but Romanization is not perfect – Korean has a wide variety of sounds not found in English, like the vowel "eu". We suggest downloading a translation app and listening to spoken Korean to perfect your pronunciation. Don't worry too much – speaking a few phrases will receive praise from the locals, and you're likely to come across some younger Seoulites who speak and understand English. That said, if you're in a traditional Korean restaurant, you'll definitely want to consult that app.

Key phrases

Learning a few phrases in Korean goes along way. Here are some to get you started.

» **Kam-sa-hab-ni-da** Thank you.

» **An-nyeong-ha-se-yo** Hello.

» **An-nyeong-hi Ka-se-yo** Goodbye (they're leaving).

» **An-nyeong-hi Kye-se-yo** Goodbye (you're leaving).

» **... ol-ma-ye-yo** How much is... ?

» **Jal Mok-oss-seub-ni-da** Thank you for the meal.

» **Soo-go-haes-seub-ni-da** You're working hard. (This is a common farewell used to thank staff.)

GETTING AROUND

Seoul is made up of 25 *gu* (districts), with the Han River flowing through its heart. Generally speaking, the north is historic (home to palaces and *hanok* villages), and the south is modern (think high-rises and malls). Sound simple? Seoul's neighborhood system is actually pretty complex. The district Dongdaemun-gu, for example, is not the same as the neighborhood Dongdaemun. And wait: Dongdaemun isn't even in Dongdaemun-gu. Standardized addresses (formatted as building number, street, district) don't mention neighborhoods, so a bar in Hongdae will only mention the district, Mapo-gu, in its address. The locals, however, do tend to refer to places by neighborhood, like Hongdae.

We know, it's a lot to wrap your head around. That's why we've provided what3words addresses for each sight in this book, so you can quickly pinpoint exactly where you're heading with ease.

On foot

Seoul's done a lot of work to make itself pedestrian friendly, having built big sidewalks and underground passages in the latter half of the 20th century. Some areas are more walkable than others, though. If you're crossing the half-mile- (1-km-) wide river, avoid the bridges and take public transportation. While Seoul is known for its fast pace, some locals are admittedly not the quickest walkers. Don't be afraid to politely announce that you're "coming through!" with a cheery *"ji-na-gal-gae-yo!"*

On wheels

Although cycling is more of a hobby than a transportation method here, bike paths make it easy to get around, with the best along the Han River. The city has an affordable public bike-sharing system, Seoul Bike, with over 3,000 docking ports; rentals start at 1,000 won per hour, and can be purchased through the English-language app.

Koreans hardly ever wear helmets (and rental bikes don't supply them) but we advise you try to wear one, all the same. Always ring your bell when you're overtaking someone, and yield to pedestrians when traveling along walking paths.
www.bikeseoul.com

By public transportation

Seoul's efficient and reliable subway – one of the most comprehensive in the world – is the pride and joy of its public transportation system. The 23 lines extend well beyond the city's perimeters, and navigating the subway is incredibly easy: signs and announcements are all offered in English, and transfer routes are intuitively placed with directional guides. Buses are just as reliable, with many offering English announcements, too.

Prices on any mode of public transportation start relatively low at around 1,300 won per trip. The easiest way to pay your fare is to get a pay-as-you-go T-Money card; buy and reload yours at any convenience store or station ticket machines. Tap in and out on both the subway and buses. Word to the wise: it's impolite to eat or speak loudly on public transportation, so best avoid doing either.

By car or taxi

Seoulites love their cars, but that means roads can easily turn into huge traffic jams – all the more reason to take buses, which have their own lanes.

When you need them, taxis are convenient and reasonable (you can even use your T-Money card to pay). Hailing them by the road works, but an app like Kakao Taxi is your best bet; you can type out your Romanized address (found online) in the app, saving you having to communicate your destination in-person in Korean.

Download these

We recommend you download these apps to help you get about the city.

WHAT3WORDS
Your geocoding friend
A what3words address is a simple way to communicate any precise location on earth, using just three words. ///quantity.donation.prices, for example, is the code for the front gate of Gyeongbokgung Palace.
Simply download the free what3words app, type a what3words address into the search bar, and you'll know exactly where to go.

NAVER MAPS
Your journey planner
Google Maps won't get you far in Korea – it's all about Naver Maps here. Available in both Korean and English, Naver gets you everywhere you need (by subway, bus, or on foot), has up-to-date subway maps, and displays transportation times down to the exact minute. Heck, it even suggests which subway door to get on for the fastest transfer.

Seoul is divided into 25 gu (districts), within which are smaller neighborhoods with their own stories to tell. Here we take a look at some of our favorites.

Seoul
NEIGHBORHOODS

Buam-dong

This tranquil neighborhood barely feels like part of Seoul, tucked as it is in the Bukhansan Mountain foothills. Here, quaint galleries and cafés share the fresh mountain air with expensive homes and sections of the city wall, not a skyscraper in sight. *{map 4}*

Bukchon

Squeezed between royal palaces, Bukchon was once the home of Joseon-era government officials. The nobility are long gone, but the narrow lanes remain lined with historic *hanok*, many of which have been converted into boutiques and cafés. It's a magnet for

tourists, yes, but it's still home to many locals who live in unconverted *hanok*. *{map 1}*

Daehangno

Thanks to a handful of universities, it's no surprise this artsy neighborhood radiates a youthful energy. Buskers croon the latest pop ballads, students rifle through flea markets, and budding actors make their name at dozens of small theaters. *{map 4}*

Dongdaemun

The area just south of Heunginjimun Gate is the center of Korea's fashion industry, home to all-night malls, wholesale markets, and Seoul Fashion Week when it comes around. It's

also the center of Seoul's Russian and Central Asian expat community, complete with Russian grocers and Uzbek restaurants. *{map 4}*

Euljiro

Decades-old factories and machine shops share Euljiro's warren of alleys with new arrivals: young creatives who've been priced out of former "it" areas, like Hongdae. These youngsters have turned vacant spaces into studios and impossibly cool bars, earning the area the moniker Hipjiro. *{map 1}*

Gangnam

Gangnam is both lauded and – as anyone who's listened to PSY's famed song knows – lampooned for its moneyed denizens, pricey real estate, and obsession with image. This is the wellspring of Hallyu and Korea's huge plastic surgery industry, and is where money is made and spent. It's hard to believe it was all a bunch of rice paddies a few decades ago. {map 5}

Hannam

This riverside neighborhood is as elite as they come, its avenues lined with swish (and expensive) apartments, chic restaurants, and classy boutiques. Little wonder K-pop stars and actors choose to live here. {map 2}

Hongdae

In the 1990s, following Korea's democratization, Hongdae grew into a font of alternative culture. Though gentrification has seen it lose some of its creative edge, with many indie businesses pushed out, the area remains a haven for artists, punks, and the LGBTQ+ community, who flock here for the ace music and nightlife. {map 3}

Itaewon

Seoul's most international neighborhood is a true community, where Turkish bakeries, American honky-tonks, and Nigerian salons have all found a place. Once a bit rough around the edges, it's now a go-to for young and LGBTQ+ crowds who appreciate its sense of freedom, with cool bars and clubs that rival Hongdae's. {map 2}

Jongno

The heart of Seoul since the 14th century, Jongno is where the past and present blend effortlessly. En route to corporate skyscrapers and government offices, workers pass royal palaces, a shrine housing the spirits of deceased Joseon kings and queens, and tourists soaking up the history. {map 1}

Seochon

Bukchon's quiet cousin, Seochon is one of Seoul's oldest neighborhoods. It's a lovely area full of handsome *hanok*, calm cafés, and traditional markets that's

blessedly overlooked by most visitors. {map 1}

Seongbuk-dong

Northwest of Bukchon, Seongbuk-dong was once home to several famous Korean writers who found inspiration in the serene hillside setting. Today, historic homes, lovely temples, and quaint teahouses provide just as much inspiration for those who come to while away the hours. {map 4}

Seongsu

Wedged between the Han River and Jungnangcheon Stream, Seongsu is one of Seoul's hottest addresses. That's especially true of areas near Seoul Forest Park — a favorite place to picnic. {map 5}

Songpa

This district's tidy grid of streets exemplifies upper-middle-class life in Seoul. On weekends, families escape their apartment towers for the green spaces of Olympic Park and Seokchon Lake. {map 6}

Seoul
ON THE MAP

Whether you're looking for your new favorite spot or want to check out what each part of Seoul has to offer, our maps – along with handy map references throughout the book – have you covered.

GOYANG

Hangang River

GANGSEO-GU

Gimpo International Airport

YANGCHEON-GU

BUCHEON

GURO-GU

GWANGMYEONG

GEUMCHEON-GU

INCHEON

0 kilometers   4
0 miles   4

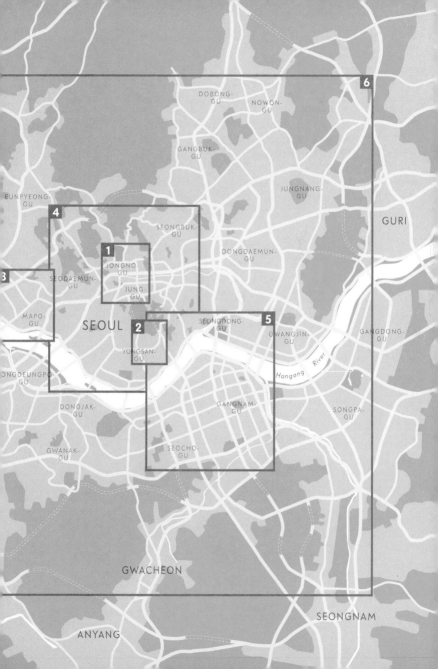

MAP 1

🅔 EAT

🅓 DRINK

🅢 SHOP

🅐 ARTS & CULTURE

🅝 NIGHTLIFE

🅞 OUTDOORS

Namsan Park

SOWOL-RO

NAMSANGONGWON-GIL

H5NG **E**

Welcome Records **S**

YONGSAN 2-GA-DONG

S Heo Sarang

Rabbithole **N**
Arcade Pub

SINHEUNG-RO

E Woorahman

SOWOL-RO

ITAEWON 2-DONG

HOENAMU-RO

Dalmaek
Super
Magpie Brewery **D** **N** **D** **N** Boogie Woogie
The Booth Brewing Company
Mr. Ahn's
Craft Makgeolli **D** **D** Gyeongnidan-gil

Leeum Samsung **A**
Museum of Art

D Namsan Sool Club

NOKSAPYEONG-DAERO

D Southside Parlor

HOENAMU-RO 44-GIL

ITAEWON-RO 27-GIL

Vinyl & Plastic
Emart24 Hannamdong **N** **S**
Tap Public **D**

N Seoul
Community Radio

ITAEWON 1-DONG

232 **D** **S** Warp
Monk's Butcher **E**

HANNAM-DONG

ITAEWON-RO

Paper/Shelter **N**

D Thursday
Party

Buddha's Belly **E**

Cakeshop **N**

N
Jeoul
Gallery

ITAEWON-RO

BOGWANG-RO 59-GIL

N Faust

N Bottoms Up

NOKSAPYEONG-DAERO

Plant **E**

YONGSAN-GU

USADAN-RO

USADAN-RO 10-GIL

SEOBINGGO-DONG

BOGWANG-RO

BOGWANG-DONG

0 meters 300
0 yards 300

MAP 2

YEONHUI-
DONG

SEODAEMUN-
GU

SUSAEK-RO

WORLD CUP BUK-RO

NAEBU EXPRESSWAY

Chaeg Bar **D**

SEONGSAN-RO

DONGGYO-RO

Greem Café **D**

SEONGSAN-
DONG

SEONGMISAN-RO-19-GIL

YEONNAM-
DONG

WORLD CUP BUK-RO

Yeonnam **S**
Bangagan

E
Moore
Cookie

N Channel
1969

Sonshinbal **S**

The War and
Women's Human
Rights Museum **A**

SEONGMISAN-RO

WORLD CUP-RO

Gyeongui Line
Book Street

NullPan **S**

Gelateria
Dangdo
E D Bokdeokbang

Kakao Friends x Gongmihak Cafe **D**

Granhand Mapo **S**
Object **S** **N**

N Mangwon
Market

SEOGYO-DONG

Gopchang Jeongol **N**

Hey
Jude I

E Mangwondong
Tiramasu

Beat Road **S**

Quafé **E**

Tokki Bar **D** **S**
D Bonchodang

D

D Mangridan-gil

Hanseam Leather Craft Workshop

Senggi **N**
Studio

Sanu
199

DONGGYO-RO

WAUSAN-RO

MANGWON-
DONG

Aland Hongdae **S**

Makgeolli Salon **D**

MAPO-
GU

YANGHWA-RO

Su Noraebang **N**

HONGDAE

KT&G Sangsang **A**
Madang

MODECi

09Women **S**

N **N** The Henz Club

Seoul Escape Room **N** **D** Vinyl Bar

HAPJEONG-
DONG

YANGHWA-RO

Cinema Four **D**

DONGMAK-RO

SEOGANG-
DONG

GANGBYEONBUK EXPRESSWAY

D Sangsu-dong

Saekdareun Hanjan **N**

D Unigorn Craft
Beer & Wine

N Chwihan Jebi

TOJEONG-RO

Yanghwa
Bridge

GANGBYEONBUK EXPRESSWAY

Seogang
Bridge

Hangang River

0 meters   500

0 yards   500

MAP 3

SINCHON-
DONG

SEONGSAN-RO

Sinchon
Hwangso
Gopchang **E** **N**

Hanshin
Pocha Sinchon

CHON-RO

E The Bread Blue

U-RO

SINSU-
DONG

DONGMAK-RO

TOJEONG-RO

E EAT

The Bread Blue *(p51)*
Gelateria Dandgo *(p56)*
Mangwondong Tiramisu *(p56)*
Mangwon Market *(p41)*
Moore Cookie *(p55)*
Sinchon Hwangso Gopchang *(p47)*
Quafé *(p55)*

D DRINK

Bokdeokbang *(p67)*
Bonchodang *(p84)*
Chaeg Bar *(p62)*
Cinema Four *(p77)*
Greem Café *(p77)*
Kakao Friends x Gongmihak
     Cafe *(p75)*
Makgeolli Salon *(p66)*
Mangridan-gil *(p72)*
Sangsu-dong *(p70)*
Sanullim 1992 *(p66)*
Tokki Bar *(p67)*
Uniqorn Craft Beer
     & Wine *(p80)*
Vinyl Bar *(p62)*

S SHOP

09Women *(p96)*
Aland Hongdae *(p96)*
Beat Road *(p108)*
Granhand Mapo *(p93)*

Hansaem Leather Craft
     Workshop *(p105)*
NullPan *(p106)*
Object *(p105)*
Sonshinbal *(p103)*
Yeonnam Bangagan *(p100)*

A ARTS & CULTURE

KT&G Sangsang Madang *(p128)*
The War and Women's Human
     Rights Museum *(p121)*

N NIGHTLIFE

Channel 1969 *(p151)*
Chwihan Jebi *(p153)*
Gopchang Jeongol *(p152)*
Hanshin Pocha Sinchon *(p139)*
The Henz Club *(p147)*
Hey Jude Bar *(p154)*
MODECi *(p146)*
Saekdareun Hanjan *(p154)*
Senggi Studio *(p152)*
Seoul Escape Room *(p142)*
Su Noraebang *(p145)*

O OUTDOORS

Gyeongui Line Book Street *(p165)*

Gilsangsa Temple **O**

Suyeon Sanbang **D**

SEONGBUK-DONG

BUAM-DONG

Bubing **E**

CHANGYEONGGUNG-R

Arko
Theat
A

Inwangsan Mountain **O**

Cheong Wa Dae **O**

La Cle **N**

SAMCHEONG-DONG

JONGNO-GU

Changdeokgung
Palace **O**

DAEHANGN

Ihwa
Mural Villag

Ansan
Jarak-gil Trail **O**

SAJIK-RO

Seodaemun
Prison History Hall **A**

SAJIK-RO

JONGNO-DONG

SAMIL-DAERO

DAEHAK-RO

Jongmyo
Park

Gwangjang
Vintage Market **S E** Gwang
Market

SAJIK-DONG

Woo Lae Oak **E**

YEONHUI-DONG

SEODAEMUN-GU

CHUNGHYEON-DONG

SOGONG-DONG

SEOUL
PLAZA

Star Samarkand

CJ The Market **S**

JUNG-GU

TOEGYE-RO

Kyungd
Presbyte
Ch

SINCHON-DONG

Ewha Campus
Complex **A**

SEOSOMUN-RO

Korea House **S**

Namsangol
Hanok Village **O**

SINCHON-RO

Yuzu Fine
Ramen **E**

Seoullo
7017 **O**

Piknic **A**

PIL-DONG

National
Theate
of Kore **A**

MAPO-DAERO

MALLIJAE-RO

CHEONGPA-RO

HUAM-DONG

Namsan
Mountain **O**

BAEKBEOM-RO

DAEHEUNG-DONG

Gongdeok Market
Jeon Alley **E E**

YONGSAN-DONG

HOENAMU-RO

MAPO-GU

Gongdeok Market
Jokbal Alley

YONGGANG-DONG

Mapo
Pocha Street **N**

BAEKBEOM-RO

Little Gangster **E**

WONHYORO-DONG

ITAEWON-DONG

Mapo
Bridge

GANGBYEONBUK

ICHON-RO

Mongtan **E**

HANGANGNO-DONG

ITAEWON-RO

YONGSAN-GU

BOGWANG-DONG

Wonhyo
Bridge

VR Zone **N**

HANGANG-DAERO

NOKSAPYEONG-DAERO

0 kilometers   1

0 miles   1

SEOBINGGO-DONG

Hangang
Bridge

National Hangeul
Museum **A**

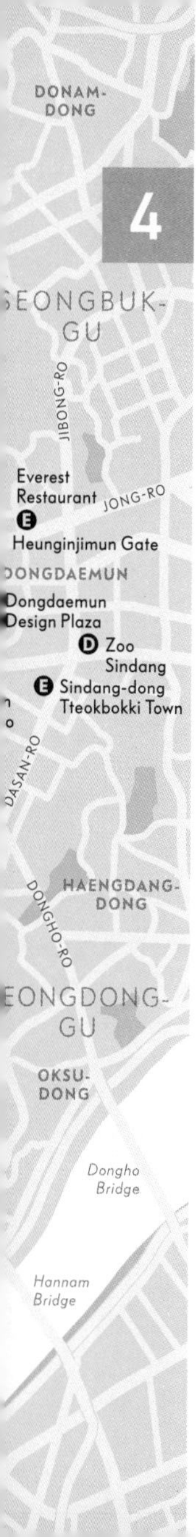

MAP 4

DONAM-DONG

SEONGBUK-GU

Everest Restaurant

Heunginjimun Gate

DONGDAEMUN

Dongdaemun Design Plaza

Zoo Sindang

Sindang-dong Tteokbokki Town

HAENGDANG-DONG

EONGDONG-GU

OKSU-DONG

Dongho Bridge

Hannam Bridge

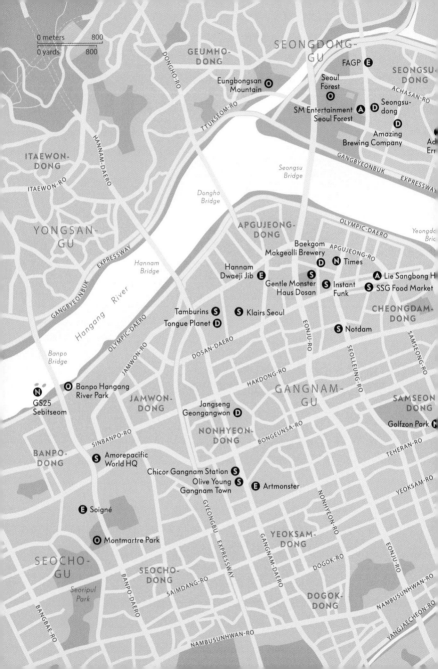

SEONGDONG-GU

GEUMHO-DONG

0 meters 800
0 yards 800

DONGHO-RO

Eungbongsan Mountain ⊙

Seoul Forest ⊙

FAGP Ⓔ

SEONGSU-DONG

ACHASAN-RO

SM Entertainment Seoul Forest ⒶⒹ

Seongsu-dong

Amazing Brewing Company Ⓓ

Ad Err

TTUKSEOM-RO

Seongsu Bridge

GANGBYEONBUK EXPRESSWAY

ITAEWON-DONG

HANNAM-DAERO

ITAEWON-RO

Dongho Bridge

APGUJEONG-DONG

OLYMPIC-DAERO

Yeongdc Bric

YONGSAN-GU

Hannam Bridge

Baekgom Makgeolli Brewery Ⓓ

APGUJEONG-RO

Ⓝ Times

Ⓐ Lie Sangbong H

GANGBYEONBUK EXPRESSWAY

Hannam Dwaeji Jib Ⓔ

Gentle Monster Haus Dosan

Ⓢ

Ⓢ Instant Funk

Ⓢ SSG Food Market

Hangang River

EONJU-RO

CHEONGDAM-DONG

SAMSEONG-RO

Tamburins Ⓢ

Ⓢ Klairs Seoul

Tongue Planet Ⓓ

DOSAN-DAERO

Ⓢ Notdam

Banpo Bridge

JAMWON-RO

OLYMPIC-DAERO

HAKDONG-RO

GANGNAM-GU

SEOLLEUNG-RO

SAMSEON DONG

Golfzon Park Ⓝ

Banpo Hangang River Park Ⓞ

Ⓝ GS25 Sebitseom

JAMWON-DONG

Jangseng Geongangwon Ⓓ

NONHYEON-DONG

BONGEUNSA-RO

SINBANPO-RO

TEHERAN-RO

BANPO-DONG

Amorepacific World HQ Ⓢ

Chicor Gangnam Station Ⓢ

Olive Young Ⓢ Gangnam Town

Ⓔ Artmonster

NONHYEON-RO

GANGNAM-DAERO

YEOKSAM-RO

GYEONGBU EXPRESSWAY

EONJU-RO

Ⓔ Soigné

YEOKSAM-DONG

Ⓞ Montmartre Park

DOGOK-RO

SEOCHO-GU

SEOCHO-DONG

SAIMDANG-RO

DOGOK-DONG

NAMBUSUNHWAN-RO

Seoripul Park

BANPO-DAERO

NAMBUSUNHWAN-RO

BANGBAE-RO

NAMBUSUNHWAN-RO

YANGJAECHEON-RO

MAP 5

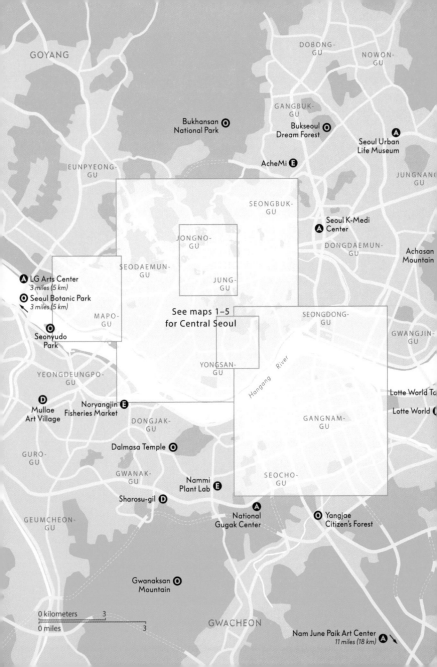

GOYANG

DOBONG-
GU

NOWON-
GU

GANGBUK-
GU

Bukhansan ◉
National Park

Bukseoul ◉
Dream Forest

Ⓐ Seoul Urban
Life Museum

EUNPYEONG-
GU

AcheMi Ⓔ

JUNGNANG-
GU

SEONGBUK-
GU

Ⓐ Seoul K-Medi
Center

JONGNO-
GU

SEODAEMUN-
GU

DONGDAEMUN-
GU

Achasan
Mountain

JUNG-
GU

Ⓐ LG Arts Center
3 miles (5 km)
◉ Seoul Botanic Park
3 miles (5 km)

See maps 1–5
for Central Seoul

SEONGDONG-
GU

GWANGJIN-
GU

MAPO-
GU

Seonyudo
Park ◉

YONGSAN-
GU

Hangang River

YEONGDEUNGPO-
GU

Lotte World To

Lotte World Ⓐ

Ⓓ Mullae
Art Village

Noryangjin Ⓔ
Fisheries Market

DONGJAK-
GU

GANGNAM-
GU

GURO-
GU

Dalmasa Temple ◉

GWANAK-
GU

Nammi Ⓔ
Plant Lab

SEOCHO-
GU

GEUMCHEON-
GU

Sharosu-gil Ⓓ

Ⓐ
National
Gugak Center

◉ Yangjae
Citizen's Forest

Gwanaksan ◉
Mountain

0 kilometers   3
0 miles   3

GWACHEON

Nam June Paik Art Center Ⓐ
11 miles (18 km) ↘

MAP 6

6

Amsa-dong
Prehistoric
Settlement Site
Ⓐ

eatre des
nieres

GANGDONG-
GU

Olympic
Park
Ⓞ   Olympic
         Ⓝ Hall

Seokcheon Lake Park
Ⓓ Songridan-gil

ch Grey

SONGPA-
GU

SEONGNAM

EAT

"Have you eaten?" is one of the most common ways to say hello in Korea, which says everything about how much food — from traditional treats to fusion feasts — means here.

Traditional Eats

Kimchi, bibimbap, kimbap: these dishes might be in hot demand across the globe today, but they're best served in Seoul. And besides, there's so much more to Korean cuisine – get ready to tuck in.

HADONGKWAN

Map 1; 12 Myeongdong 9-gil, Jung-gu; ///wacky.lobster.trailing; www.hadongkwan.com

Restaurants in Seoul come and go at lightning speed, so the fact that Hadongkwan made it through the Korean War, the 1997 Asian financial crisis, and urban redevelopment is testament to how good it is. Since 1939, workers have been staving off the winter chills here with a comforting bowl of *gomtang*: a soup of beef and rice seasoned to taste. It's simple but perfect, and perfection keeps you in business.

STORY OF THE BLUE STAR

Map 1; 17-1 Insadong 16-gil, Gwanhun-dong, Jongno-gu; ///dwarves.urge.treat; 02-734-3095

Choi Il Soon might be a celebrated theater actor here in Seoul, but it's his organic food restaurant that steals the show. And Choi wouldn't have it any other way: he'd sooner wax lyrical about the locally sourced tofu on the menu, or where he found the perfect *makgeolli* brew for his bar, before mentioning his latest stage venture. Besides, the huge *jeon* (Korean style pancakes) provide enough to talk about.

» **Don't leave without** pairing the fresh *makgeolli*, served in traditional dented pots, with your *jeon*.

SAN CHON

Map 1; 30-13 Insadong-gil, Jongno-gu; ///sponge.darkest.bend; www.sanchon.com

When Buddhist Jeong Kwan spoke about Korean temple food on Netflix's *Chef's Table* in 2017, the world became obsessed with clean eating. But to the people of Korea, it's nothing new: monks and nuns have followed a plant-based diet, as prescribed by Buddhist philosophy, for 1,700 years, and you'd be forgiven for thinking San Chon has been open just as long. Run by a former monk, this temple food spot is highly celebrated for its seasonal dishes, cooked without additives and seasoned with mountain herbs. Nightly performances, from shamanic dances to Buddhist ceremonies, top off your dinner.

Try it!
TEMPLE FOOD CLASS

Known for its simple flavors, Korean temple food often excludes pungent aromatics like onions. Learn why at the Korean Temple Food Center *(www.koreatemplefood.com)* while cooking up your own subtle dish.

GONGDEOK MARKET JOKBAL ALLEY

**Map 4; start at exit 5 of Gongdeok Station, 19 Mallijae-ro, Mapo-gu;
///business.grant.rise**

Your cardiologist might not be happy if you visit this alley, but your dermatologist will be; *jokbal* (pork trotters boiled in soy sauce) is thought to be great for the skin, since the tender pig feet are high in collagen. Hit up any of the many *jokbal* joints in Gongdeok Market to give it a try, making sure to order *sundae* (blood sausage) soup and a bottle of soju to wash it all down.

TOSOKCHON SAMGYETANG

**Map 1; 5 Jahamun-ro-5-gil, Jongno-gu; ///lined.eats.predict;
www.tosokchon.com**

Seoulites swear by the health benefits of *samgyetang*, a soup that contains a small chicken stuffed with rice, ginseng, nuts, jujubes, and garlic. It's traditionally eaten on *sambok*, the three hottest days of the

There's arguably no one better to learn about North Korean food from than Lee Ae-ran, a defector who founded an institute for the study of such food *and* restaurant Neungra Bapsang (*www.neungra.com*).

This small spot serves dishes you'll almost never find on this side of the DMZ, like Kaesong *mu-jjim* (steamed radish) and Pyeongyang *onban* (chicken soup with rice). It also provides jobs for female defectors.

year. Sound like a recipe for a sweaty disaster? That's the point. It's believed that the soup's heat balances your body temperature with the temperature outside, while the ingredients replenish the nutrients you need. It's on these hot days that you'll find the biggest crowds tucking into steaming bowls at Tosokchon, which has occupied a renovated *hanok* since 1983.

YURIMMYEON

Map 1; 139-1 Seosomun-ro, Jung-gu; ///picture.memo.vets; 02-755-0659
Arguably, the best restaurants in Seoul have been serving one dish, and one dish only, for decades. At Yurimmyeon, it's buckwheat noodles. For over 50 years, the matriarchs helming this family-run restaurant have been making the noodles from scratch, drawing lunchtime lines that wind round the block. Order by the season: cold noodles in the summer, warm in the winter.

WOO LAE OAK

Map 4; 62-29 Changgyeonggung-ro, Jung-gu; ///shopper.inner.fountain; 02-2265-0151
This institution has been dishing up many variations of *naengmyeon*, a buckwheat noodle dish, since 1946, but it's the Pyongyang-style *naengmyeon* that has people obsessed. A North Korean specialty, this dish consists of cold buckwheat noodles topped with thin strips of pear, kimchi, and beef in a tangy, refreshingly cold broth.
» Don't leave without also ordering some meat dishes. This spot is known for its bulgogi (marinated beef) and *galbi* (marinated ribs).

Street Food

Fast, cheap, and often made by the city's finest cooks, street grub is at the heart of Seoul's food scene. It's hard to resist the warm glow of a market or the aromatic steam emanating from a tiny stall.

MYEONGDONG NIGHT MARKET

Map 1; Myeongdong-gil, Jung-gu; ///divider.scan.views

As soon as 5pm hits this fashion district, the streets heave with over 150 vendors tempting hungry shoppers. You'll find the usual street food suspects like fried chicken and *tteokbokki* here, but it's the experimental dishes that you'll be itching to try. Ever considered grilled cheese lobster? What about Nutella-filled fish-shaped bread? A spiral-cut potato on a skewer (also known as a tornado potato)? There's a stall for each of these and more.

GONGDEOK MARKET JEON ALLEY

Map 4; 1st floor, Gongdeok Market, 23 Mallijae-ro, Mapo-gu;
///airbag.soldier.sage; 02-712-0076

Jeon – savory fried pancakes – are the ultimate home-style Korean comfort food, and have been the star of this market alley since the 1980s. Can't decide between *jeon* flavored with mung bean, kimchi,

Raining outside? Pair your *jeon* with the local *makgeolli* – a rainy day tradition in Korea.

or mushroom? Try them all. You pay according to weight here, so simply fill a wicker basket (it's more like a plate) with whatever you want to try.

GWANGJANG MARKET

Map 4; 88 Changgyeonggung-ro, Jongno-gu; ///scores.paves.touches; www.kwangjangmarket.co.kr

Korea's first permanent market is an oil-streaked paean to street food. It's held onto its roots as a haunt for workers to convene after a long day, some of whom recall coming here in the post-Korean War years for a cheap yet filling feed. Let the steam from noodle vats and the sizzle of *bindaetteok* (mung bean pancakes) wash over you while you navigate the cramped stalls, lined with benches where businessmen, students, and tourists sit shoulder to shoulder.

NORYANGJIN FISHERIES MARKET

Map 6; 674 Nodeul-ro, Dongjak-gu; ///dare.padlock.measures; www.susansijang.co.kr

Seoul's largest fish market is a wet wonder, populated by booted workers hawking the likes of mackerel, squid, and clams. If you'd rather eat your chosen catch on-site, tell the vendor and head to one of the upstairs restaurants, where the staff will turn your purchase into sashimi or spicy *haemultang* (seafood soup).

» Don't leave without trying *san-nakji*, small octopus that's chopped up and served – still wiggling – with sesame oil and a dipping sauce.

SINDANG-DONG TTEOKBOKKI TOWN
Map 4; 10-18 Dasan-ro 33-gil, Jung-gu; ///weedy.credited.remodel;
02-2236-9135

No matter where in Korea they're from, everyone grew up eating *tteokbokki*: soft, chewy rice cakes simmered in a red chili paste sauce. Stalls selling the snack are everywhere, but this alley is where the spicy version of *tteokbokki* got its start back in 1953, when Ma Bok-Lim (owner of Maboklim Tteokbokki and affectionately known as the "Godmother of Tteokbokki") accidentally dropped a rice cake into her father's noodle bowl. Realizing how good it tasted, she formulated a new seasoning for the snack, and popularity was immediate. Today, numerous restaurants along this alley follow in her footsteps, serving their own take by adding ingredients like cheese and black bean sauce.

» Don't leave without trying Maboklim Tteokbokki's *tteokbokki*, of course. This unique blend of red chili pepper paste with Chinese soybean paste is the original formula, and it's hands down the best.

TONGIN TRADITIONAL MARKET
Map 1; 18 Jahamun-ro 15-gil, Jongno-gu;
///pebble.wing.broom; 02-722-0911

Seoul's street food markets have always been community gathering places, where neighbors catch up and stressed workers forget the day over affordable grub. Tongin was established in 1941 for this very reason – initially as a base for Japanese residents during the occupation, then open to everyone after the Korean War. Though it's become decidedly less local and more touristy in the last decade, tradition is still at the heart of Tongin, with real currency exchanged for replica *yeopjeon* brass coins that were used during the Joseon era – a reminder of what life was like before modernization. Use your coins to buy an empty lunch box, load it with quick bites such as *dakgangjeong* chicken and stir-fried anchovies at participating stalls (they'll have a sign), and tuck in at the second floor dining room.

NAMDAEMUN KALGUKSU ALLEY

Map 1; 42-1 Namdaemunsijang 4-gil, Jung-gu;
///winter.zoom.concerts

This alley might be located in Namdaemun – one of Seoul's biggest shopping markets – but it still feels like a well-kept secret. As soon as you open its plastic doors, the (mostly) female stall owners usher you in with warm smiles, loud shouts, and the heavenly scent of *kalgusku*, a knife-cut noodle broth dish. Each stall has its own secret recipe, but the lips of the cooks are sealed (apart from when they're enthusiastically yelling at you to choose their stall, that is).

MANGWON MARKET

Map 3; 27 Poeun-ro 6-gil, Mapo-gu; ///snaps.lovely.someone;
www.mangwonsijang.modoo.at

Delightfully off the tourist trail, Mangwon exists primarily as a hub for Mapo residents, which means no tourist price mark-ups here. The market provides a snapshot of local life, where workers hunt for dinner groceries, couples grab rice donuts for a picnic at the nearby Han River, and friends settle at the sit-down restaurants for bibimbap.

Global Grub

*Korean cooking will always reign supreme in Seoul,
but there's a huge appetite for international food, too.
Many restaurants cater to, and reflect, the city's
immigrant communities from Asia and beyond.*

SOIGNÉ

**Map 5; 46 Banpo-daero 39-gil, Seocho-gu; ///question.slip.insurers;
www.soignerestaurantgroup.com**

Fusion food is everywhere in Seoul, whether it's spicy rice cakes that
ooze cheese or the use of a chili paste and cream rosé sauce. This
two-Michelin-starred, reservations-only restaurant does fusion a
little more elegantly with its French-Italian-Korean menu, which
changes according to the featured local ingredient – maybe Asian
pears with chamomile, or seasonal fish with water parsley.

YUZU FINE RAMEN

**Map 4; 53-8 Mallidong 1(il)-ga, Jung-gu; ///finally.coconut.boost;
070-4177-0365**

You can easily find more than 10 types of *ramyeon* (Korean instant
noodles) at any convenience store, so many locals consider Japanese
ramen an upgrade. Yuzu Fine Ramen gives this perennial favorite a

Enjoy a free refill of the broth and noodles when you order the signature yuzu *shio* or shoyu ramen.

distinctively Korean spin, with yuzu fruit – commonly used to make a sweet tea – included in the broth. Time to forgo the grocery store noodles, we say.

STAR SAMARKAND

Map 4; 14 Eulji-ro 42-gil, Jung-gu; ///panics.nowadays.says; 02-2279-7780

"Little Russia," an area within the neighborhood of Gwanghui-dong, is something of a misnomer; it's also home to Uzbekistan, Kazakhstan, and Mongolian joints set up by migrants. Star Samarkand is one such place, where the comforting scent of slow-cooked lamb emanates off traditional Uzbek plateware. In the chill of winter, hearty staples like steamed pies and meaty soups – washed down with strong liquor – are a tonic for homesick expats.

» **Don't leave without** trying the *samsa* – a savory pastry baked fresh in an Uzbek clay oven.

BUDDHA'S BELLY

Map 2; 48 Noksapyeong-daero 40-gil, Yongsan-gu; ///trouser.warnings.taker; 02-796-9330

Debates on Seoul's best Thai spot are as long as pad thai is popular (very). Bypass the local disputes and listen to the Thai government instead: Buddha's Belly has been certified by its program, Thai Select, which aims to promote authentic Thai cuisine across the globe. Expect quality curries, *tom yum goong*, and pad thai, of course.

FAGP

**Map 5; 136 Wangsimni-ro, Seongdong-gu; ///results.splat.vibrate;
02-6052-7595**

Freaking Awesome Good Pasta lives up to its whimsical name. In
the open kitchen, chefs use dried seaweed or black bean to jazz up
humble pasta, making you rethink everything you thought you knew.

» Don't leave without trying homemade pickles alongside your pasta
(it's not a Korean experience without a fermented veggie side dish).

EVEREST RESTAURANT

**Map 4; 2-1 Jong-ro 51ga-gil, Jongno-gu; ///blazers.clubs.plates;
www.everestfood.com**

Not even the colorful lanterns or catchy Bollywood tunes playing
from the TV could distract from the creamy curries at Everest, one of
Seoul's original spots for Nepalese and Indian food. Reading through
the list of veggie, seafood, chicken, and mutton curries alone takes
a while, so try one of the set menus to taste the bestsellers.

H5NG

Map 2; 95-17 Sinheung-ro, Yongsan-gu; ///jingles.melon.spoon

A hole-in-the-wall Chinese restaurant inside Sinheung Market,
H5NG is one of those places where the food manages to be of
great value without compromising taste. There's only room to seat a
handful of people, making it an intimate space where regulars come
often to enjoy the likes of Szechuan eggplant and lemon chicken
cooked by the owner, who runs the place completely on his own.

Liked by the locals

"Seoul's food culture is hard to pinpoint – trends rise and fall at a meteoric pace. But the growth in appetite for international foods, often imported by foreign-trained chefs, is a trend that's likely to continue."

JAMES CHUNG, PHOTOGRAPHER AND
LOCAL FOOD ENTHUSIAST

Meat Feasts

Koreans are unabashed carnivores. The smoky smell of cooked meat along every street is a sign that you're never far from a fried chicken or BBQ joint – with some serving dishes that aren't for the faint of heart.

ARTMONSTER

Map 5; 28-3 Teheran-ro 1-gil, Gangnam-gu;
///hangs.dusted.tramps; www.artmonster.co.kr

Also known as KFC, Korean fried chicken is the ultimate fast comfort food, found anywhere and everywhere people need a good feed. What makes this neon-lit spot stand out from other franchises is its

Shh!

There's no reason to miss out on Korean fried chicken if you're not a meat eater. Maru Jayeonsik Gimbap (*1st floor, 35–4 Insadong-gil, Jongno-gu*) is a tiny stall located in a shopping mall – something you'd easily overlook if you weren't on the hunt. The staff here proudly wear aprons stating "EAT VEGAN," and serve up vegan fried chicken that gives the meaty equivalent a run for its money.

killer atmosphere, always buzzing with friends dropping in on a night out. Order a craft beer to pair with your fried chicken – so beloved a combo that it's birthed a whole new word, *chimaek*.

HANNAM DWAEJI JIB

Map 5; 21 Apgujeong-ro 28-gil, Gangnam-gu; ///swatted.homes.awake; www.hanampig.co.kr

K-BBQ first timer? This is the ideal place to cut your teeth. As a general rule at BBQ joints, you cook your own meat over tabletop grills, but Hannam Dwaeji Jib takes that pressure away. Choose your meat (the set menu gives a mix of the most popular cuts) and the staff will pre-cook it over a charcoal fire for a smoky taste. They'll then monitor, grill, and cut your meat for you, telling you when it's ready to eat. All that's left for you to do is enjoy your meal.

SINCHON HWANGSO GOPCHANG

Map 3; 31 Yonsei-ro 9-gil, Seodaemun-gu; ///shots.update.proofs; 02-337-2640

Gopchang (offal) BBQ isn't for everyone, but it's a local delicacy, and this decades-old spot does it best. After a long day, office workers huddle around sizzling plates of beef and pig, waiting for the rich, fatty meat to turn golden brown. Come with a translation app or a Korean-speaking friend to explain the intricate parts of offal you didn't know existed, like the heart and large intestine.

» Don't leave without finishing off with fried rice and a shot of soju for the truly local, full-course event.

WOORAHMAN

Map 2; 25 Sowol-ro-38-gil, Yongsan-gu; ///cycles.velocity.roses;
02-797-8399

Korean BBQ is usually a pretty casual affair, but Woorahman offers a cut above the rest. This upscale spot is *the* place to come for Hanwoo: beef from a native breed of cattle, known for its fine marbling, tender texture, and irresistible flavor. It's also expensive, so trips to Woorahman are often reserved for special occasions. Splurge on a tasting menu and one of the chefs will grill the beef at your table, serving it with elevated versions of classic *banchan* (side dishes).

» Don't leave without asking for the whisky pairing option; Woorahman has an impressive collection to accompany each dish.

MONGTAN

Map 4; 50 Baekbeom-ro 99-gil, Yongsan-gu;
///staging.stand.conquest; www.mongtan.co.kr

When the staff tell you they're all booked up by noon, they're not joking; so popular is this meat joint that locals stand in line from 10am to make a dinner reservation. Why? Mongtan offers *udae galbi* – a rare prime cut of large beef ribs that's absolutely delicious.

HWAYUKGYE

Map 1; 21 Eulji-ro 14-gil, Jung-gu; ///winners.create.option

Join those burning the midnight oil at Hwayukgye, a laid-back restaurant serving *yasik*, or late-night food. Chicken feet are a classic snack in Seoul, and Hwayukgye serves them at three different spice levels; depending on how brave you're feeling, try the spiciest level 3. Marinated with garlic, soy sauce, a *lot* of red chili pepper, and a closely guarded secret ingredient, they might just blow your head (or feet) off.

JONGNO GALMAEGISAL ALLEY
Map 1; Start at Exit 6 of Jongno-3-ga Station;
///enforced.gender.empires

Whatever you can think of — books, cafés, savory pancakes — Seoul probably has an alleyway dedicated to it. But it's the city's meat alleys, often tucked between densely packed buildings, that get the most love. Take Jongno Galmaegisal Alley. The pungent smell of stew, mixed with beer and soju, hangs in the air along this boisterous narrow alley, where unironically retro signs haven't changed since the 1990s. At the cluster of restaurants lining the alley, diners gather at outdoor tables, grilling their own meat over charcoal grills before wrapping the meat, rice, kimchi, garlic, and seasonings in lettuce, then wolfing down the whole thing in one bite.

Try it!
MASTER SOME MEAT

Want to cook fried chicken the Korean way? Or maybe learn a stir-fried pork recipe? Whatever dish you want to make, Food & Culture Academy *(www.koreanrecipe.co.kr)* will teach you how on a day course.

Veggie and Vegan

Seoul is a meat-eater's city, there's no doubt about it. But times are changing and, led by a new generation of foodies, plant-based spots are slowly getting the attention they deserve.

JINJUHUIGWAN

Map 1; 26 Sejong-daero 11-gil, Jung-gu; ///lush.brass.doormat; 54-682-0608

First time experiencing Seoul's muggy summer heat? You'll be thankful for a trip to Jinjuhuigwan, where cold soybean noodles are served vegan and with sweet kimchi if you ask for no meat. Since it's only available in the summer months, lines can be long, but don't be deterred: you'll be slurping it all down in no time.

OSEGYEHYANG

Map 1; 14-5 Insadong 12-gil, Jongno-gu; ///gearbox.dolphin.trash; www.go5.co.kr

To live like a local is to eat like one, but with a flavor palate as meat heavy as Korea's, it can be difficult to find authentic options that are also plant-based. Osegyehyang is an exception to the rule, offering vegan versions of iconic local dishes – black bean noodles, kimchi stew, tofu "chicken" – in a rustic *hanok*. It's run by Ching Hai, an advocate of veganism from the Guanyin Famen school of Buddhism. Yes, this school is often described as a "cult," but rest assured no one is trying to convert you to anything here other than delicious food.

THE BREAD BLUE
Map 3; 3 Sinchon-ro 12da-gil, Mapo-gu; ///singing.welcome.press; www.thebreadblue.com

Tucked between two major universities, this vegan bakery and café is a haven for students needing a quick bite. Here, the stimulating aroma of freshly baked vegan cookies and just-brewed coffee (dashed with soy, almond, or oat milk, which are difficult to find even in big-name chains) keeps the energy up between classes.

MONK'S BUTCHER
Map 2; 228-1 Itaewon-ro, Yongsan-gu; ///claims.deflection.haunts; 02-790-1108

Vegan fine dining is hard to come by in Seoul, where the plant-based scene is mostly made up of casual lunch spots. That's what makes this dinner spot – the kind you need to reserve ahead at – a standout. Inside, ambient lighting adds warmth to the marble stone walls, and friends sit elbow to elbow on rustic wooden tables. As for the food, expect a hearty mix of dishes ranging from pumpkin gnocchi to coconut curry.

» Don't leave without heading to the sister business, Monk's Deli, in Haebangchon for lighter lunch fare.

Solo, Pair, Crowd

Whether you're indulging alone or hunting for food that makes everyone happy, Seoul has you covered.

FLYING SOLO
Scribble with a scrambled
ByTOFU, in Haebang-chon, is a tiny shop that's practically designed for solo diners looking to write in their diaries. It's hard to find a vegan scrambled egg like the one served here in Seoul – or anywhere, really.

IN A PAIR
Eat your veggies
Cozy and intimate, Base is Nice in Mapo-gu lends itself perfectly to a catch-up. Book ahead to enjoy skillfully crafted Korean dishes with ingredients such as charcoal-grilled corn and lotus root.

FOR A CROWD
One of everything, please
Gathering the gang but everyone has different dietary requirements? Satisfy them all at Ssong Thai in Itaewon, which serves both plant-based and meat Thai dishes such as curry and pad thai.

NAMMI PLANT LAB

Map 6; 55 Bangbaecheon-ro 4an-gil, Seocho-gu;
///chairs.saints.drifting; 02-522-1276

Columbian Christian Oviedo first visited Korea to learn more about Asian food, and after falling in love with the country, decided to move here. What did he learn about the food on his travels, you ask? Well, that plant-based options were lacking, which led to the opening of Nammi. Expect organic dishes like bulgogi pizza and spicy rice.

PLANT

Map 2; 117 Bogwang-ro, Yongsan-gu; ///inherit.brains.influencing;
www.plantcafeseoul.com

Mention veganism in Seoul and most locals will scream "Plant!" – not a reference to "plant-based," but a reflection of just how popular this vegan joint is. This trendy spot full of plants (apt) is a hit with the most carnivore of carnivores, who lap up the varied menu of Mexican fajitas, sesame peanut soba bowls, and big salads.

LITTLE GANGSTER

Map 4; 11-3 Saechang-ro 12-gil, Yongsan-gu; ///narrow.sport.supple;
02-3272-4058

This snug spot packs a punch. Not only does it add Korean twists to Eurasian dishes, like kimchi cream risotto, it also puts a vegan spin on traditionally meat-heavy foods, like the spicy noodle soup laksa.
» Don't leave without striking up a chat with the English-speaking owner, who's always happy to share her journey into vegan chef-hood.

Sweet Treats

A gooey cookie with a morning coffee, a crunchy rice donut after school, a pot of red bean ice cream during a night out: when it comes to indulging in the sweet stuff, anything goes.

ACHEMI

Map 6; 82 Sungin-ro 2-gil, Seongbuk-gu; ///drones.faces.snapped; 02-6409-0011

Finding plant-based ice cream in Seoul is no easy feat, so when vegans stumble upon AcheMi, they feel as if they've hit the jackpot. And they have. Not only is its rice milk-based ice cream *oh so* smooth and creamy, the creative flavors change by the season – perhaps camellia flower in the summer and sweet potato in the fall.

BUBING

Map 4; 136 Changuimun-ro, Jongno-gu; ///motels.corded.owners; 02-394-8288

Seoul's hot and humid summers call for *bingsu*, a dessert of shaved ice that dates all the way back to the Joseon era. It's typically mixed with condensed milk and paired with toppings like seasonal fruits and red beans, and Bubing does it the best – the lines are as big as the portions here. Oh, and an added bonus? Bubing sells *bingsu* year-round, so you can enjoy over 20 flavors of the sweet stuff even if you're not sweating in the summer.

QUAFÉ

Map 3; 8 Hongik-ro 6-gil, Mapo-gu; ///window.tenses.sounds;
www.quafe.kr

Back in the 1970s, it was practically unheard of to pass through a market without picking up a *kkwabaegi*. Crunchy on the outside, soft on the inside, these twisted rice donuts were the perfect pick-me-up. The retro desserts fell out of fashion at the start of the 21st century, but places like Quafé have revived interest, giving them a modern makeover with flavors like salted caramel and toppings like cheese and crackers.

MOORE COOKIE

Map 3; 250 Donggyo-ro, Mapo-gu; ///same.limo.flames;
10-8273-4910

For some, comfort food after a long day is a hearty kimchi stew; for others, it's a warm, buttery cookie. If you fall into the latter camp, you need Moore Cookie, a great big hug of a bakery serving everything from a classic chocolate chip to a lemon earl grey flavor. You can get one to-go, but we suggest enjoying it in the café, since the staff will heat your chosen cookie up for extra gooey goodness.

» **Don't leave without** trying the honeycomb cookie, topped with locally sourced honey, a crunchy honeycomb, and soft cream cheese.

OLD FERRY DONUT

Map 2; 66 Hannam-daero 27-gil, Yongsan-gu; ///hype.comet.lays; 02-6015-2022

So dedicated to the humble donut was Old Ferry Donut owner Choi Min-yi that she traveled across the US on the hunt for the best flavors, baking techniques, and ingredients. The result is the first bakery in Seoul to use a 12-hour fermented yeast dough for its iconic flavors, which include loaded peanut butter and "cream" brulée.

MANGWONDONG TIRAMISU

Map 3; 87 Poeun-ro, Mapo-gu; ///tokens.blame.zone; www.mangtira.com

Okay, tiramisu is not a born-in-Korea dessert, but it incorporates coffee – a necessity in daily life here, hence its popularity. Individual tiramisu servings, with seasonal flavors like cherry blossom, are sold in paper cups, perfect for a sweet treat on the go.

» **Don't leave without** ordering a milk tea. This creamy drink paired with an original tiramisu is a match made in heaven.

GELATERIA DANGDO

Map 3; 106 Poeun-ro, Mapo-gu; ///biked.fried.penny; 70-8690-1088

Locals will tell you that a dessert only tastes as good as it looks (it has to photograph well for social pages, right?). This gelateria gets the idea, serving its homemade gelato in cups with animal faces drawn on, topped with two scoops to mimic ears. It's almost too cute to eat. (Almost.)

Liked by the locals

"Find any bakery in Seoul and you will feel the detailed care that goes into every item. From extravagant desserts to simple but classic pastries, Seoul has it all."

MEENA HWANG, OWNER OF LOCAL ONLINE BAKERY
BAKE ME HOME

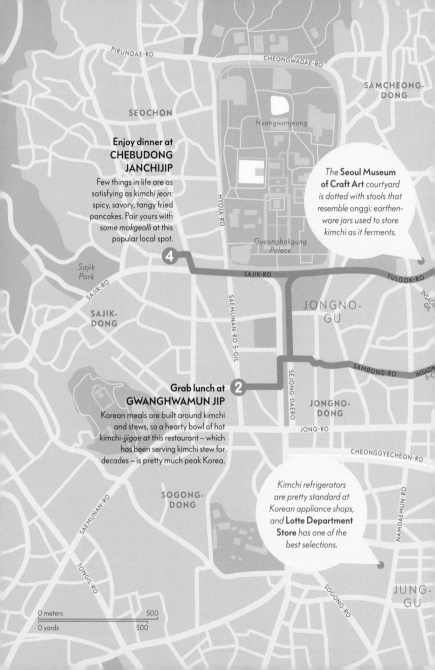

PIRUNDAE-RO

CHEONGWADAE-RO

SAMCHEONG-
DONG

SEOCHON

Hyangwonjeong

HYOJA-RO

**Enjoy dinner at
CHEBUDONG
JANCHIJIP**

Few things in life are as
satisfying as kimchi *jeon*:
spicy, savory, tangy fried
pancakes. Pair yours with
some *makgeolli* at this
popular local spot.

*Gyeongbokgung
Palace*

The **Seoul Museum
of Craft Art** courtyard
is dotted with stools that
resemble onggi: earthen-
ware jars used to store
kimchi as it ferments.

*Sajik
Park*

SAJIK-RO

YULGOK-RO

INSA...

4

SAJIK-
DONG

SAEMUNAN-RO 5-GIL

JONGNO-
GU

SEJONG-DAERO

SAMBONG-RO

INSA...
5-C

**Grab lunch at
GWANGHWAMUN JIP**

Korean meals are built around kimchi
and stews, so a hearty bowl of hot
kimchi-*jjigae* at this restaurant – which
has been serving kimchi stew for
decades – is pretty much peak Korea.

2

JONGNO-
DONG

JONG-RO

CHEONGGYECHEON-RO

SAEMUNAN-RO

SOGONG-
DONG

Kimchi refrigerators
are pretty standard at
Korean appliance shops,
and **Lotte Department
Store** has one of the
best selections.

NAMDAEMUN-RO

TONGIL-RO

JUNG-
GU

SOGONG-RO

0 meters   500

0 yards   500

Map labels

GAHOE-DONG

3 **Make your own at SEOUL KIMCHI ACADEMY**
Kimchi is complex, but making it isn't hard. This school in a tile-roofed house will show you how to do it, and then vacuum-pack your kimchi to take home.

GYEDONG-GIL

YULGOK-RO

SAMIL-DAERO

JONGNO-DONG

Do your research at MUSEUM KIMCHIKAN
Hit up this kimchi museum to learn about the dish's history and all the varieties it comes in. You can even peer at its healthy bacteria through a microscope.

CHEONGGYECHEON-RO

EULJIRO-DONG

EONG-ONG

A day exploring Seoul's
kimchi culture

Ah, kimchi. Think of it as just a side dish and you'll miss how central it is not only to Korean cuisine but to Korean culture, too. This spicy, sour, umami treat is a key part of every meal here, and there are over 200 varieties (yup, you read it right) to choose from beyond the standard napa cabbage. The ancient practice of *kimjang*, making kimchi in preparation for winter, is still an important custom, and just about every family has their own recipe (not to mention kimchi refrigerator for proper fermentation, of course). Feeling hungry yet? Here's where to experience Seoul's favorite food.

1. Museum Kimchikan
35-4 Insadong-gil, Jongno-gu;
www.kimchikan.com
///fade.cutaway.gossip

2. Gwanghwamun Jip
12 Saemunan-ro-5-gil,
Jongno-gu; 02-739-7737
///contents.pounding.tips

3. Seoul Kimchi Academy
102 Gyedong-gil, Jongno-gu;
www.kimchischool.net
///polo.recount.mediate

4. Chebudong Janchijip
16 Jahamun-ro-1-gil,
Jongno-gu; 02-730-5420
///canine.paints.fakes

Lotte Department Store
///bunks.fashion.cable

Seoul Museum of Craft Art
///airtime.plot.magazine

DRINK

To really see all sides of Seoul, sip your way through the city. Enjoy a creative coffee in a quirky café, savor a calming tea in a quiet den, and shoot some soju at a rowdy bar.

Cocktail Joints

Seoul's creative side comes out to play in its cocktail bars. Unusual concoctions, wacky themed settings, and inventive ways of serving a well-mixed drink define the city's cocktail scene.

VINYL BAR

Map 3; 61-1 Wausan-ro, Mapo-gu; ///points.gushes.camped; 02-322-4161
No, this isn't an LP bar – the "vinyl" in the name is actually the Korean word for "plastic." At this tiny hole-in-the-wall, classic and original cocktails are served in zip-lock plastic packs, perfect for sipping en route to a club. Think of it as juice for your journey.

CHAEG BAR

Map 3; 24 Yeonhui Mat-ro, 101, Seodaemun-gu;
///buffoon.donates.savings; 02-6449-5858
This cozy literary bar has one rule: "Keep calm and drink a book," and it couldn't be easier to follow. Firstly, group entry is maxed at three, speaking loudly is barred, and jazz music plays faintly in the background – all pretty calming. But how do you drink a book, you ask? Well, the mixologists whip up cocktails that feature in iconic novels, like a Gin Rickey from *The Great Gatsby* or a Cutty Sark

highball from *1Q84* – they can even tell you which chapter the drinks are in. Enjoy yours with your nose in a book, naturally.

» **Don't leave without** pressing a small button attached to a sliding bookshelf door to access a whole other room with a bar.

JANGSENG GEONGANGWON

Map 5; 23 Gangnam-daero 124-gil, Gangnam-gu; ///trickle.soils.boarded; 10-2278-5968

Traces of this building's past life as a "health center," where healthy juices were concocted using herbal medicines, are still tangible at this "healthy bar." That doesn't mean you can expect cocktails that won't result in a hangover (unless you opt for a non-alcoholic type). Rather, it means drinks made with traditional medicinal ingredients like chili peppers, ginseng, and bellflower. The bar makes the most of its location in Yeongdong Traditional Market, too, collaborating with a different vendor each month to create a new cocktail (previous mixes have seen *tteokbokki* and *naengmyeon* on the menu).

232

Map 2; 232 Itaewon-ro, Yongsan-gu; ///sport.padlock.clearing; www.232.co.kr

This classy bar hidden in a Hannam basement might be on the pricier side, but its distinct brand of Seoul cool makes it worth spending the won. If the 1950s decor, vinyl record system, and high-end cocktails aren't enough to win you over, the famous DJs and K-pop producers playing mellow sets at the bar will.

BAR SOOKHEE MYEONGDONG

Map 1; 4th floor, 7-9 Myeongdong 10-gil, Jung-gu;
///passport.legwork.gold

On the fourth floor of a nondescript building, an antique mirror with a discreet "open" button on the frame is the only hint that something lies beyond. And what a something it is. Press the button to enter the 1920s time capsule, where dapperly dressed bartenders whip up custom cocktails and couples make eyes over rare whiskies.

SOUTHSIDE PARLOR

Map 2; 4th floor, 218 Noksapyeong-daero, Yongsan-gu;
///depend.double.cracker; www.southsideparlor.com

Yes, the cocktails are innovative and the no-frills bar food is comforting, but it's the Southern hospitality that's made this bar a firm favorite among Itaewon locals. Southside Parlor was opened by a group of Texan expats, and they never fail to make customers

You'll struggle to find Our's Cafe and Bar *(Yanghwa-ro 6-gil 99-9, Mapo-gu)* on Google, so consider this your "in." Founded by a barista and a bartender, this bar unites what Seoulites love the most: coffee and alcohol. Coffee-infused cocktails – Irish martinis made with espresso, cold-brew negronis – keep catch-ups going into the small hours (as does the home-baked cookie platter).

feel at home, whether they're catching up with regulars while mixing them an old-fashioned or advising area newbies on where to go for a night out. Monthly drag brunches, weekday trivia, and charity events for rescue dogs add to the community vibes.

>> **Don't leave without** trying a signature cocktail, which include mixtures such as scotch with sherry, fermented soy, and *makgeolli*.

ZOO SINDANG

Map 4; 411 Toegye-ro, Jung-gu; ///molars.pebble.chipper; 02-2231-1806

Are you a rat? A tiger? Maybe a snake? If you don't know what we're on about, you'll quickly find out after visiting this Lunar zodiac-themed bar, where the menu is split by the 12 signs, identifying the drinks that best represent each one. To enter, turn the head of a cat (ironically not one of the 12 Lunar zodiac animals) and leave the evening in the hands of your sign. Monkey? Expect a cocktail of white rum, peach juice, and lemon. Rooster? It'll be a hibiscus vodka with egg white concoction for you. You get the idea.

JEAN FRIGO

Map 4; Toegye-ro 62-gil, Jung-gu; ///pull.settle.premiums; 02-2275-1933

It's a speakeasy tale as old as time: enter through a refrigerator door inside what looks like a fruit shop, place your order on a retro public phone, and cozy up on a sofa while your drink is prepared. In keeping with the theme, all cocktails are fruit-based, ranging widely in both sweetness and alcohol levels (including none at all).

Traditional Drinks

For a real taste of Korea, you need to be sipping on home grown spirits, from sweet rice wines like soju to specially fermented brews like **makgeolli***. These are the places to seek out the good stuff.*

SANULLIM 1992

Map 3; 60 Seogang-ro 9-gil, Mapo-gu; ///chilled.seating.kitten; 02-334-0118

Sanullim 1992's vibe is pure country *jumak* (tavern), with brass kettles, wicker baskets, and horsehair hats hanging from the walls. That country warmth extends to its staff, who provide the perfect introduction to Korean spirits. Tell them what you're after – fizz, fruity notes, the savoriness of burnt rice – and they'll pick from the 200 varieties of craft and small-batch soju, *makgeolli*, and other alcohols.

MAKGEOLLI SALON

Map 3; 12-6 Wausan-ro 21-gil, Mapo-gu; ///scorch.friends.expires; 02-324-1518

For centuries, *makgeolli* was seen as little more than "farmer's liquor," drunk before a day's work in the fields. But over the last decade, the milky-white fermented rice wine has seen a resurgence, and places like Makgeolli Salon are leading the charge. This bar showcases *makgeolli* from all over Korea, so you can sip brews made in Goyang City, Dangjin, and Seoul all in one night.

>> Don't leave without ordering a *makgeolli* blended with fresh fruits. The liquor is pretty tangy already, but this mix is ideal for a sweet tooth.

TOKKI BAR

Map 3; 4th floor, 130 Yanghwa-ro, Mapo-gu;
///spider.stepping.hedge; www.rysehotel.co.kr/tokki_bar

Rivaling *makgeolli* for Korea's number one spirit is soju: a distilled alcohol, almost like a sweeter vodka, that's drunk neat. It's found in almost every bar in Seoul, but Tokki is the only place serving its own American-produced soju (no cynicism, please: it really is as good as the made-in-Korea stuff). The Tokki brand got its start in NYC, which explains the Brooklyn-inspired, sultry speakeasy vibes at its Seoul outpost. Expect exclusive cocktails made with in-house soju, served under the gentle glow of dim lights. Perfect for a date, we say.

BOKDEOKBANG

Map 3; 5 Poeun-ro 8-gil, Mapo-gu; ///aquatic.gross.deep;
070-8864-1414

Bokdeokbang means, roughly, "house of generous hosts," and this intimate bar is the closest you'll come to a night at a Korean home. Your generous hosts are a mother-and-son team – mom cooks up dishes like tofu and aged kimchi, while son makes pairing suggestions from the bar's selection of natural *makgeolli* from around the country.

Solo, Pair, Crowd

No matter where you are in the city, you're never far from a bar that's passionate about local liquor.

FLYING SOLO
Cocktail for one

A negroni with soju? Yes please. Bar Cham in Jongno is the place to cozy up with a unique cocktail, made with Korean spirits sourced from across the country.

IN A PAIR
Cheers to a catch-up

Go all out for a BFF get-together at SanSol, a restaurant serving *makgeolli* that's made in small breweries across Korea. The tables are small and intimate, perfect for chatting over dinner with a tipple.

FOR A CROWD
Get a round in

Kickstart your night out at Neurin Maeul Brewery and Pub, where your gang can choose from a range of spirits – including *makgeolli* and *cheongju* – to pair with delicious *anju* like boiled pork. Stomachs full, it's onto the next place.

MR. AHN'S CRAFT MAKGEOLLI

Map 2; 3 Hoenamu-ro, Yongsan-gu; ///adopting.captive.forgets;
10-5172-2229

Snacks – known as *anju* – are often ordered alongside drinks in
Seoul, and Mr. Ahn's serves some of the best. Enjoy your *makgeolli*
with seasonal plates like beef brisket croquettes and hamachi sashimi.
» Don't leave without trying the *takju* (unrefined rice wine) and
cheongju (refined rice wine) for a deeper dive into Korean alcohol.

NAMSAN SOOL CLUB

Map 2; 228-2 Noksapyeongdae-ro, Yongsan-gu;
///float.closet.enigma; 0507-1326-3921

Have no idea where to begin with *sool* (Korean alcohol)? Unsure if
you prefer a spicy or bitter flavor? American-Canadian sommelier
Dustin opened this bar just for you. Okay, it was more to develop
everyone's interest in local liquor, but the staff are so attentive, you'll
feel as if you're the only customer. They'll pour and chat you through
some of the 80 by-the-glass options until you find love at first sip.

BAEKGOM MAKGEOLLI BREWERY

Map 5; 39 Apgujeong-ro 48-gil, Gangnam-gu; ///yappy.agent.breezy;
www.whitebear.modoo.at

This two-story bar is the place to be on the weekend, when trendy
locals scan the shelves for a new drink to try – it stocks over 200
varieties of traditional liquor from around Korea, after all. When
it inevitably gets too crowded, take your chosen tipple outside.

Café Streets

So loved is coffee here that locals call Korea the Coffee Republic. Entire streets are dedicated to the humble coffee shop, with places opening and closing with alarming regularity (that's rising rents for you).

SANGSU-DONG

Map 3; start at 70 Dongmak-ro, Mapo-gu; ///troubled.obstruction.referral

The cafés lining this district's alleys are more than places to get a brew: they're gathering spaces for Hongdae's creatives, who all have their favorite bohemian spot to spend the day working in. For many, that's Yri Café – one of the first coffee shops to open in the area in 2009, and *remain* open even as new places have come and gone nearby. Settle in among the writers leafing through the café's second-hand books and the musicians enjoying the mellow records.

MULLAE ART VILLAGE

Map 6; start at 54-37 Mullaedong 3(sam)-ga Yeongdeungpo-gu; ///defers.finishing.enjoyable

Art and industry sit side by side in this neighborhood, which explains its unique aesthetic: working factories, dusty alleys, and colorful murals. Seek out those murals by zig-zagging through the tiny

Note that some cafés only open in the early evening to avoid factory noise during the day.

alleys, popping into cafés lining them as you go. Look for the most iconic café of all: Rust Bakery, which sells croissants and coffee in an industrial building.

SHAROSU-GIL

Map 6; start at 111 Gwanak-ro 14-gil, Gwanak-gu; ///loans.miss.egging

The students of Seoul National University (SNU) have a reputation for being *very* studious, and this relatively short street has become their sanctuary, the varied cafés along it providing space for every occasion. Need to get your head down? Head to Ongojisin, where talking is always a whisper. Curious what life after graduation is like? Visit Saesil Garden Cafe, a former butcher's shop transformed by two SNU architecture graduates. Simply after some strong caffeine? Order a Yemen Mocha Matari at Cafe Sanda.

SEONGSU-DONG

Map 5; start at 656-320 Seongsu 1(il)-ga, Seongdong-gu; ///breeding.magma.myself

Known as Seoul's Brooklyn, this shoe manufacturing district has seen cafés slowly take over its former warehouses. But aside from its cool aesthetic, Seongsu-dong's draw is its proximity to Seoul Forest. If you need some caffeine before walking the park, forgo the popular (read: packed) Cafe Onion and get a refreshing tea from Matchacha.

» Don't leave without visiting Cha to try its Korean honeycomb-flavored desserts and drinks – a flavor made famous by *Squid Game*.

SONGRIDAN-GIL

Map 6; start at 23 Baekjegobun-ro 43-gil, Songpa-gu;
///spits.works.corals

Being trendy in Seoul doesn't just relate to what you wear or who you listen to, but where you hang out too. And this upscale street is where locals go to be seen; even its fancy cafés prioritize aesthetics over bean quality. New spots pop up all the time, but PRES Coffee is a constant favorite for its rooftop views of Lotte Tower (just mind the snap-happy influencers up here).

GYEONGNIDAN-GIL

Map 2; 3 Hoinamu-ro, Yongsan-gu; ///masters.mission.collide

It's worth the workout to navigate this steep street: every café along it serves incredible coffee, often made using high-quality beans from global importers. If we had to pick a top spot, it'd be Everything But the Hero, for its intensely flavored hand-drip selections.

» Don't leave without visiting Berkeley Coffee Social; dog owners and their pooches often pop by after a morning walk on nearby Mt. Namsan.

MANGRIDAN-GIL

Map 3; 105 Poeun-ro, Mapo-gu; ///smokers.cashier.ladder

For Seoul's retirees, a morning stroll along the Han River always seems to end at a café along this street. Yes, it's in Hongdae, which is known as the center of "youth culture," but the range of cafés here – from time-honored haunts to mainstream roasteries – truly offers something for everyone.

Liked by the locals

"Café streets are all about finding moments of rest in a busy schedule, embracing the little things in life, and, of course, enjoying a truly good cup of coffee."

ALLISON NEEDELS, TRAVEL WRITER
AND HISTORIAN

Themed Cafés

Robot baristas, turn-of-the-century antiques, comic book illusions: Seoul's themed cafés make you feel as if you've transcended time, space, and even dimensions. Life's too short for a boring coffee shop.

PEACH GREY

Map 6; 2nd floor, 24 Baekjegobun-ro 41-gil, Songpa-gu;
///canyons.loser.rocker; 0507-1334-1693

For a city that's constantly on the move, it's important to find somewhere to slow down and recharge, and this watercolor café is the perfect place to do just that. Every drink option – be it a watermelon smoothie or a strawberry-topped latte – comes with a set of watercolors, brush pens, and paper, so you can while away the hours painting between sips of something sweet.

ART X SHIFT

Map 1; 5th floor, 54-17 Chungmu-ro Jung-gu;
///acting.splint.stapled; www.artxshift.com

The brainchild of artists Zachary Roberts and Ah-young Jeon, this experimental gallery café is like peeking inside their imagination. Every year, the artists take turns to reimagine the decor – one

 Check out Art x Shift's socials to see if it's hosting any of the classical music concerts it's known for.

season it might feature bright cartoon drawings, the next only purple and blue hues. Order a homemade lavender latte and take in the artistry of the place.

KAKAO FRIENDS X GONGMIHAK CAFE

Map 3; 3rd floor, 162 Yanghwa-ro, Mapo-gu;
///denote.wages.polished; 0507-1374-334

You're in Seoul, so you've probably got the KakaoTalk app to message your mates. And, if you *do* have it, you'll be using the Kakao Friends emoticons. Okay, some hate them, but many more love the likes of Muzi, a playful radish in rabbit clothes, and Angmond, a chocolate-loving harp seal. This café inside the Kakao Friends store sure does, serving up lattes almost as sweet as the characters themselves.

BOT BOT BOT

Map 5; 8 Achasan-ro 9-gil, Seongdong-gu; ///partied.warriors.popular;
www.botbotbot.kr

It's common to see human tasks taken over by automation in Korea. No one bats an eyelid at the robots behind Bot Bot Bot's counter, like Dripbot making hand-drip coffees with precision and Drinkbot stirring up cocktails. Don't worry; human staff are on hand to take orders and work alongside their robot co-workers, a sign of how automated technology has been wholly embraced in the city.

» Don't leave without choosing a custom pattern for the café's third robot employee, Dessertbot, to draw on your cake.

TONGUE PLANET

Map 5; 518-11 Sinsa-dong, Gangnam-gu;
///fled.graced.blacked; www.tongueplanet.com

Tongue Planet is a terrific example of the somewhat muted quirkiness and eccentricity of Seoulites, rarely seen on the homogenous streets of trendy areas like Gangnam. Coming in here is to enter a fever dream, as is trying to describe the place. Tongues are ... everywhere. Picture subtly curved tables, mirrors, and trays, and tongue-shaped cookies and neon signs by the counter. What's more, there's actually more than one of these places. It's the Sinsa branch that has tongues wagging the most, with its huge stone tongue model by the entrance that was *made* for posing beside. To access this branch, register on the website to gain a password (here's hoping it's not a tongue twister) and once you're in, order a milky coffee topped with a chocolate powder tongue. Ready to get a pic with the statue? Stick your tongue out for good measure.

Shh!

Sometimes, the best themed cafés are the simplest, like retro Coffee Hanyakbang *(16-6 Samil-daero 12-gil, Jung-gu),* hidden away in a narrow alley. Exquisite Korean-style vintage furniture and one-of-a-kind tableware fill the two-floor café, dotted with delightful little touches like a rotary telephone and an organ-style piano. Order a hand-drip coffee, made using beans roasted by hand, and see what other eccentricities you can spot while you sip.

GREEM CAFÉ

Map 3; 10-161 Seongmisan-ro, Mapo-gu;
///coconut.wounds.airless; 10-2612-8103

Ever imagined stepping into a comic book? This immersive café is way ahead of you, inspired by the Korean TV series *W*, in which characters from the real world and the webtoon universe collide. It's cleverly designed so that everything looks like a 2D drawing on paper, with only the outlines of the white furniture painted in black – an effect that's so surreal, it feels as if the floorboards will give way as you walk, the chairs will collapse when you sit down, and the knives and forks will crumble if you cut your milk roll. (They won't.)

>> Don't leave without ordering a flower shake topped with a cartoon-esque flower, since taking photos is banned until you buy something.

CINEMA FOUR

Map 3; 3-3 Dongmak-ro 9-gil, Mapo-gu; ///agrees.elated.stud;
www.cinema4.co.kr

Movie buffs can – and oh do they – spend all day in this café/cinema/shop. While you browse the DVDs and posters for sale with meticulous detail, a film (chosen by the owner) will be playing on a projector on the lower mezzanine level. Want to sit and enjoy it? You'll have to order a drink at the bar. If it's a romantic Korean movie, the owner might suggest a sweet coffee for you; if it's a Hollywood horror, he'll prompt you toward an alcoholic drink to get through the scaries; and if it's *Harry Potter*, he'll strongly advise you order a butterbeer (well, what else?). Ask for English subtitles if it's a domestic foreign language film that's playing.

Bars and Breweries

Though beer arrived in Korea in the early 20th century, it's only in the last decade that Seoul's beer scene has boomed. The city is now a thriving craft beer capital, with an ever-growing array of breweries.

MAGPIE BREWERY

Map 2; 244-1 Noksapyeong-daero, Yongsan-gu;
///stutter.handed.remote; www.magpiebrewery.com

Prior to 2012, Seoul and craft beer didn't exactly go hand in hand, with the scene solely dominated by lager brands like Hite. That was until Magpie Brewery's Canadian owners spotted a gap in the market for North American-style brews. They began experimenting with international hops on nearby Jeju island before opening this

Try it!
CRAFT YOUR OWN BEER

Why leave brewing to the experts? Visit Seoul Homebrew (*www.seoulhomebrew. com*) to stock up on all the gear you'll need to brew your own, along with handy tips on crafting your own porters and IPAs.

bar – the first in Seoul to serve a sour beer. Magpie has been on the up ever since, and its name is now synonymous with the city's craft beer scene. Expect a lively assortment of expats and locals at the Itaewon bar, hankering for that sweet, hoppy goodness.

>> **Don't leave without** trying one of Magpie's seasonal drinks, which could be a blackberry and cacao sour ale or a floral German lager.

TAP PUBLIC

Map 2; 244 Itaewon-ro Twin Bldg, Yongsan-gu; ///topmost.saying.pimples; www.tappublic.com

Though alcohol is typically served with food in Korea, it's not frowned upon if you forgo ordering snacks with your beer at Tap Public – in fact, the beer here is so good, it's all you'll need. Housing a vast assortment of self-service beer taps, this is the perfect spot to sample new flavors, like a Peanut Butter Milk Stout or local Itaewon Pale Ale. Nurse your chosen pint in the Hannam branch's beer garden.

THURSDAY PARTY

Map 2; 6 Itaewon-ro 27-gil, Yongsan-gu; ///device.carting.limes; 82-2322-0063

This well-loved franchise of dive bars knows exactly what it's good at: decent beer, and lots of it. If you like some healthy competition with your pint, choose Thursday's raucous outpost in the exchange student hub of Hongdae, which comes complete with dart boards and beer pong tables. Come for the beer, stay for the party.

UNIQORN CRAFT BEER & WINE
Map 3; 35 Dongmak-ro 2-gil, Mapo-gu;
///strapped.precautions.instance; 070-4222-4198

This bar's colorful entrance, illuminated with pink and aqua lights, offers a tantalizing promise of the welcoming atmosphere within. Proudly LGBTQ+-friendly, Uniqorn is an all-out celebration of love in its many forms. At no other bar in Seoul can you peruse a choice selection of sex toys along with a local array of organic wines. Oh, and did we mention the impressive beer selection? Uniqorn's vegan craft brews change monthly, and all have memorably defiant names, from Feminista IPA to Love Wins Wheat Ale. Whatever brings you to the eye-catching entrance, it's good vibes only inside.

» Don't leave without seeking some four-legged friends. Famously pet-friendly, the bar lets drinkers bring their canine companions – see, it's welcoming to all.

THE BOOTH BREWING COMPANY
Map 2; 7 Noksapyeong-daero 54-gil, Yongsan-gu;
///soup.chucks.arrow; 050-71370-4723

The Booth Brewing Company's co-founder Daniel Tudor famously wrote in *The Economist* in 2012 that "brewing remains just about the only useful activity at which North Korea beats the South." But it needn't remain so. A year later Tudor decided to intervene and teamed up with beer-loving mates – one a former investment analyst, another a doctor, no less – to kickstart this neighborhood bar. Suffice to say it was a success, with the people of Seoul arriving not only for the great beer but for the city's finest pizza, too. (Fun fact: a pizza plus beer is known as a *pimaek* here in Korea.)

KIWA TAPROOM

Map 1; 74-7 Yulgok-ro 1-gil, Jongno-gu;
///formally.audible.journals; 02-733-1825

This *hanok*-style taproom, named after the Korean word for traditional roof tiles, distinguishes itself from the city's rowdier beer spots with its peaceful and subdued atmosphere. Visit in the day and sunlight beams down on the courtyard, perfect for relaxing over a cool pint. It has one of the city's best selection of beers, too. The list changes frequently, but Mungyeong Brewery's Jeomchon IPA is a regular fixture; one sip, and you'll see why.

AMAZING BREWING COMPANY

Map 5; 4 Seongsuil-ro 4-gil, Seongdong-gu;
///declares.spoken.disposal; www.amazingbrewing.co.kr

Yes, this brewpub is as amazing as its name so clearly states. Grab a wristband upon entry, pick a glass, and hit up any of the 50-plus self-service beer taps. Partial to a darker beer? Go for the raspberry milk stout, Dark Ambition. Prefer something sweet? Opt for the Cherry Wheat Ale. Unsure what flavors you're into? Never fear: quality beer education is integral to the company's mission, so pick up some refined tasting tips at its brewing talks (the schedule is posted on the website).

Teahouses

Koreans have been drinking tea since the Silla era, and show no signs of being bored of the stuff. It's sipped all day and all year in delightful teahouses, sanctuaries from the frenetic pace of modern life.

SHIN OLD TEAHOUSE

Map1; 47-8 Insadong-gil, Jongno-gu; ///goats.shows.altering; 02-732-5257

Tucked in a back alleyway, this little teahouse is worlds away from the lively Insadong streets just around the corner. Inside, friends sit cross-legged on floor cushions, whispering over steaming cups of tea served with complimentary rice cakes. If it's warm out, bask in the sunshine on the green courtyard; if it's not, stay cozy inside and watch the birds flutter outside the large windows.

O'SULLOC TEAHOUSE BUKCHON

Map 1; 45 Bukchon-ro, Jongno-gu; ///totally.direct.warrior; www.osulloc.com

O'Sulloc is a big name in Korea's tea industry, its fragrant tea from the Seogwang Tea Fields in Jeju often gifted among locals for birthdays and anniversaries. So, this three-story teahouse is something of an O'Sulloc nirvana: a place to shop for said gifts on the first floor, taste a cup of green tea on the second, and finish off with a "teatail," like a Jeju tangerine tea-ade, at the bar on the third.

TEA THERAPY

Map 1; 74 Yunposun-gil, Jongno-gu; ///lamp.requires.pillows; 02-730-7507

Are you a perfectionist? Have cold hands and feet? Hardly drink any water? There's a tea for you. Tea Therapy firmly believes that tea is, well, therapeutic; take a self-diagnosis test, full of questions like those we've just asked, and the color-coded menu will direct you to teas with (supposedly) beneficial medicinal properties. Not so keen on taking a test? Simply ask the staff for recommendations.

» Don't leave without paying a small fee for the outdoor foot bath during the warmer months. Traditional Korean medicine believes warm feet help keep the body healthy, so give those toes a treat.

TTEURAN TEAHOUSE

Map 1; 17-35 Supyo-ro 28-gil, Jongno-gu; ///fidget.fracture.convert; 02-745-7420

Those who stumble upon this quaint teahouse can't help but feel like they've uncovered a little secret — much like the owner, who bought the *hanok* back in 2009 after falling instantly in love with its rustic interior and vine-dappled courtyard. While she prepares handmade snacks, cradle a cup of traditional *omijacha* (tea made from red berry), sunlight streaming through the huge windows.

DELPHIC

**Map 1; 84-3 Gyedong-gil, Jongno-gu; ///central.ranked.grouping;
www.delphic.kr**

Don't fret, you haven't come to the wrong place – there really is
a tearoom inside this concrete building, on the second floor to
be precise. Rustic *hanok* vibes are swapped out for a minimalist
aesthetic here: exposed brick ceilings, a sleek tea ceremony counter,
and long wooden tables displaying modern tea sets. It's really stylish,
much like the creatives who come for a milky oolong before visiting
the (equally minimalist) gallery on the floor below.

YEONHWAJEONG

**Map 1; 15-3 Insadong-gil, Jongno-gu; ///brave.typhoon.luggage;
www.yhtea.co.kr**

It's said that tea originated in China's Yunnan province, and
Yeonhwajeong is Seoul's specialty spot for a taste of its pu'er tea (or
boyicha in Korean). The fermented, bitter tea is known to aid digestion
and improve blood circulation, and as such is often enjoyed by elderly
locals in this antique little teahouse.

BONCHODANG

**Map 3; 2nd floor, 7 Hongik-ro 2-gil, Mapo-gu;
///braked.latched.nurture; 010-7371-2936**

Bonchodang is the teahouse equivalent of a trendy coffee shop –
a vast space with high industrial ceilings, thriving plants, and comfy
sofas. The tea menu is just as huge and comforting, split into themes

that indicate what each tea can offer you. Take "Beauty," which has teas like the "S-line" and "V-line" that claim to help maintain a slim figure or sharp jawline. Or "Health," where a "Hongdae Club Tea" supposedly relieves a hangover, and a "SSanghwa cold tea" might prevent a cold. Don't expect miracles, but do expect to spend an entire afternoon here, sinking into a sofa with a brew and a cake.

SUYEON SANBANG

Map 4; 8 Seongbuk-ro 26-gil, Seongbuk-dong, Seongbuk-gu; ///outgoing.received.risk; 02-764-1736

Once the home of local author Lee Taejun, Suyeon Sanbang aptly means "a small house in the forest where writers meet." It's easy to see why he was so inspired to use the setting in his stories: tucked away on a sloping hill and surrounded by trees, it's as serene as it gets. Come with a notebook and order a citrusy *yujacha* and you may find yourself inspired to write, too.

» Don't leave without trying the pumpkin shaved ice in the summer. Suyeon Sanbang was the first place to serve this subtly sweet delicacy.

Try it!
TEA OMAKASE

Indulge in a three-course tea *omakase* (chef's choice) at Gallery the Square, where seasonal dishes are made to pair with green, white, and black teas. Reserve via the coffee shop's social channels.

A morning sipping Korea's
classic drinks

Korea's drinks menu extends far beyond the green tea and soju we all know and love. Seoul's favorite tipples range from ancient spirits rooted in tradition to fresh takes on foreign imports, each offering an insight into a different side of Korea. Ceramic cups of dandelion tea in cozy teahouses conjure days gone by; convenience store shelves packed with bottles of sugary pop nod to the fast pace of city life; and creative caffeinated concoctions served in stylish cafés showcase the city's youthful cosmopolitanism. There's no better way to experience this multifaceted city than by sampling its many classic drinks.

1. Emart 24
68 Samcheong-ro,
Jongno-gu; 070-7700-2750
///gliding.stared.amuse

2. Samcheong-ro
///motivations.zooms.found

3. The Sool Gallery
18 Bukchon-ro, Jongno-gu;
www.thesool.com
///detection.flagged.paddock

4. Tea Therapy
74 Yunposun-gil, Jongno-gu;
www.teatherapy.com
///wiped.expert.anchors

National Folk Museum of Korea
///shortage.nickname.tuned

Cha-Teul
///howler.trees.track

Get a caffeine fix along SAMCHEONG-RO

This gingko-lined road is full of impeccably designed cafés. Choose one to while away a few hours at, reading a book with a coffee and a cake.

Rise and shine at EMART 24

Pop into this convenience store for a Banana-mat Uyu (banana-flavored milk) or Bacchus-D, the energy drink that Koreans swear is the ultimate hangover cure.

Cha-Teul serves tea in a pretty hanok, with huge windows that look out on Inwangsan and Bukhansan mountains.

GAHOE-DONG

With shaded benches and open-air exhibits, the National Folk Museum of Korea is a lovely place to enjoy your morning drink.

SAMCHEONG-DONG

BUKCHON-RO 5-GIL

BUKCHON-RO 4-GIL

SAMCHEONG-RO

Savor a cup at TEA THERAPY

Koreans have long used tea as medicine, and this café and clinic continues the tradition. While your tea leaves steep, enjoy a foot bath – all part of the health-centric experience.

Get into the spirit at THE SOOL GALLERY

Learn all about soju and other traditional spirits at this *sool* (Korean alcohol) museum. It also hosts tastings, so make sure you arrive thirsty.

SAMCHEONG-RO

BUKCHON-RO 5GA-GIL

BUKCHON-RO

NGWADAE-RO

ngwonjeong

ongbokgung
Palace

SEJONG-DAERO

JONGNO-GU

JONGNO-DONG

SAJIK-RO

INSADONG-GIL

SAMIL-DAERO

0 meters   250
0 yards   250

1

2

3

4

SHOP

It takes a lot to coax a city of avid online shoppers in-store, but Seoul manages it. With AR beauty counters and DJs playing as you browse, shopping isn't just about spending.

Beauty Buys

From ten-step routines to fermented ingredients, it's safe to say Koreans are serious about their skincare. And they dream big, crafting an ingenious beauty scene that makes use of the latest technology.

OLIVE YOUNG GANGNAM TOWN

Map 5; 429 Gangnam-daero, Seocho-gu; ///transfers.money.coached; www.oliveyoung.co.kr

If you've trawled K-beauty trends online, you'll know about Korea's "glass skin" effect: a hydrated, dewy complexion. It's achieved by layering products like moisturizers, cleansers, and essence – all of which can be picked up at Korea's best cosmetics chain, Olive Young. The three-story Gangnam Town location is ten steps above the rest, since it hosts special pop-ups with brands like Dr.Jart+ and Solgar.

AMOREPACIFIC WORLD HQ

Map 5; 100 Hangang-daero, Yongsan-gu; ///seats.grades.panics; www.apgroup.com

Whether it's combining AI with facial detection tech or using 3D printers to create personalized sheet masks, Korea leads forward-thinking skincare. Amorepacific is a case in point, having used pioneering scientific methods (like launching the world's first green tea cosmetic products in 1989) from its very start. What's more, at the brand's HQ, you can snap a picture of yourself on an AR mirror to be recommended specific products. How's that for futuristic?

CHICOR GANGNAM STATION
Map 5; 441 Gangnam-daero, Seocho-gu; ///scanner.envy.haven; www.chicor.com

At this cosmetics megastore, a scan of the scalp with a handheld machine is all that's needed for the staff to generate your new hair-care routine. New shampoo in the bag? Head to the color studio, where a color expert (yep, it's a thing) identifies the perfect shade of make-up and clothes for your skin tone. You'll leave with a whole new understanding of yourself – just reserve ahead first.

AMORE SEONGSU
Map 5; 7 Achasan-ro 11-gil, Seongdong-gu; ///plot.united.chapels; www.amore-seongsu.com

If K-beauty advocates anything, it's that products should be tailored to the individual. It's what this space – owned by the Amorepacific brand – was built on, with a Beauty Library that lets you test over 2,000 products for free. Make-up artists are on hand to help, but you'll want the assistance of the AR cameras, which detect your skin type and create customized lipsticks and foundations based on your results.

≫ Don't leave without enjoying a calming tea from the O'Sulloc café on the second floor, which has gorgeous views over Seoul.

Solo, Pair, Crowd

Even if you're not that into your skincare or make-up, Seoul will have you embracing the fun of self-care.

FLYING SOLO
Treat yourself
Seoulites don't stop at the face when it comes to skincare. The flagship store for skincare brand Sulwhasoo in Gangnam is also a spa, so enjoy an anti-aging back treatment before shopping for products.

IN A PAIR
Blowout with a bestie
Why wait for a special occasion to get a makeover? Enjoy the full K-celeb treatment – hair styled, make-up done, nails painted – while catching up with a pal at Jenny House Cheongdam Hill.

FOR A CROWD
Bond in a bathhouse
It's not a proper trip to Korea until you've gone to a 24-hour *jjimjilbang* (bathhouse) after a long night out. Gather the gang at Club K Seoul in Gangnam and replenish in red clay, ice, and salt rooms.

KLAIRS SEOUL

Map 5; 44 Nonhyeon-ro 153-gil, Gangnam-gu;
///noses.embodied.patting; www.klairs.com

Demand for products that align with climate-conscious lifestyles
is growing in Seoul, and eco-friendly brands such as Klairs are
responding in kind. In this flagship store, clean, vegan products
(ideal for sensitive skin) line minimalist shelves, and recycling
campaigns encourage a growing awareness around sustainability.

GRANHAND MAPO

Map 3; 9 Wausan-ro 37-gil, Mapo-gu; ///fooling.mull.trees;
www.granhand.com

Granhand opened in 2014 with a mission: to invite locals to make
fragrance a part of their everyday, not just special days. They've done
this by combining mild scents with the Gen-Z desire to customize
everything. Choose a bottle and get your initials engraved onto it.

» Don't leave without trying the Susie Salmon hand cream, a
fragrance that's described as "a midday nap after eating sweet fruits."

TAMBURINS

Map 5; 44 Apgujeong-ro 10-gil, Gangnam-gu;
///mops.backward.charm; www.tamburins.com

When Tamburins launched its first perfume in 2022 endorsed by
BLACKPINK's Jennie, beauty buyers flocked to this gallery-esque
store. They've hardly left since, coming to spritz the cult perfume
while checking out the brand's toners, hand creams, and serums.

Street Style

International brands, the rise of K-pop, and a new generation's desire to express individuality have done wonders for Seoul's street fashion. It's all about mixing cutting-edge brands with the odd vintage piece.

ADER ERROR

Map 5; 82 Seongsuyi-ro, Seongdong-gu; ///refrain.admiral.ranks; www.en.adererror.com

This skater-style brand isn't into labels. Rather, its unisex clothing line reflects the younger generation's refusal to conform to gender expectations. Ader Error prizes self-expression — much like the social media influencers who flock here for new season releases, mixing and matching everything from ripped jeans to graphic hoodies to create their perfect outfit.

INSTANT FUNK

Map 5; 12 Dosan-daero 51-gil, Sinsa-dong, Gangnam-gu; ///slurred.resort.match; www.instantfunk.kr

Korea's "Newtro" trend — a combination of new and retro — has fully infiltrated Seoul's fashion world, and helped Instant Funk become an instant hit. The brainchild of designer and stylist Kim Jihye, this

Rather do all your shopping under one roof? Head to the Times Square Mall to browse local brands.

higher-end streetwear store stocks casual staples inspired by retro designs of the 1980s and 90s. Think baggy pants, funky crop tops, and oversized cardigans.

WARPED

Map 2; 26 Itaewon-ro 42-gil, Yongsan-gu;
///nursery.personal.party; www.warped.co.kr

You don't come to Warped just to buy streetwear; you come to suss out the hoodies *and* potential collaborators for your next music project. The beats (courtesy of a DJ owner) that pulse through the store draw creatives, who come to chat ideas with the owner and those hanging by the counter. It's located in one of Seoul's trendiest back alleys, so rest assured there's a bar nearby to discuss that project further.

GENTLE MONSTER HAUS DOSAN

Map 5; 50 M floor, Apgujeong-ro 46-gil, Gangnam-gu;
///divides.approve.bake; www.gentlemonster.com

In 2011, Gentle Monster was born out of the local demand for oversized sunglasses with nose bridges suited to Asian faces. And that demand has only grown since, with this huge store opening in 2021. The three-floored space showcases minimalist eyewear and bold sunglasses collections alongside quirky art installations, embodying the brand's mission to push the norms.

» Don't leave without exploring the Haus Dosan building, which includes the Nudake dessert café on the basement level.

GWANGJANG VINTAGE MARKET
Map 4; 2nd floor, 88 Changgyeonggung-ro, Jongno-gu;
///wicked.tripled.employer; 02-2267-0291

Forget the overpriced boutiques in Hongdae; this is Seoul's original source for well-curated vintage finds, like cashmere sweaters in mint condition and luxury brand jackets. Come with cash, since many vendors are willing to give you a discounted cash price if you buy in bulk (as if you needed more reason to stock up).

09WOMEN
Map 3; 1st floor, Unit 101, 64 Yanghwa-ro, Mapo-gu;
///crawler.discount.diverts; www.en.09women.com

A dress might be labelled "one size fits all," but it rarely does in Seoul; in fact, it's most likely a small or extra small. That's what makes 09Women a breath of fresh air – its casual sweatshirts, flowing dresses, and cute lingerie are sold in a range of sizes, for a range of women.

ALAND HONGDAE
Map 3; 29 Yanghwa-ro 16-gil, Mapo-gu; ///steadily.sublet.wept;
www.aland.forbiz.co.kr

If Seoul street style was captured in shop form, it'd be Aland. Here, the likes of vintage coats brush up against modern, fresh sneakers, all from a mix of domestic and international brands.

» Don't leave without browsing the accessories, including phone popsockets or grips – considered an extension of personal style.

Liked by the locals

"Seoul street style used to be regional, like Gangnam hip-hop versus Gangbuk retro. But now, mixing and matching is in everywhere – it's considered hip to juxtapose vintage or domestic brands with luxury labels rather than wear luxury head to toe."

KWON MIN-JI, DIGITAL DIRECTOR OF *VOGUE KOREA*

Foodie Gifts

Korean food is made for sharing, so do just that and pick up some ingredients and kitchen tools to take back home (and to sate those Korean food cravings when they inevitably hit).

DOKKAEBI HANGWA GANGJEONG

Map 1; Tongin Market, 16 Jahamun-ro-15-gil, Jongno-gu; ///contacts.shelved.families; www.1902seochondokaebi.modoo.at

This confectionery outlet sells *gangjeong*, traditional sweets of puffed grains, seeds, nuts, and beans mixed with starch or rice syrup (think of it like a denser, stickier, more savory Rice Krispie Treat). Famously soft and sugar- and preservative-free, Dokkaebi's can be bought as single-ingredient or mixed bars stuffed with the likes of almonds or brown rice. Free samples are on hand to help you make up your mind; mixed gift sets are available if you inevitably can't.

CJ THE MARKET

Map 4; 330 Dongho-ro, Jung-gu; ///over.calm.nuggets; www.cj.co.kr

CJ CheilJedang is one of Korea's largest food companies, its tofu and frozen dumplings found in supermarkets across Korea, as well as in this exclusive Seoul shop. If you're keen to give family members the staple ingredients that Seoulites have in their own pantries – gochujang (red chili paste), dried seaweed, pre-made packs of *naengmyeon* (cold noodles) – CJ's got you covered.

>> **Don't leave without** surprising friends back home with CJ's Korean takes on Western staples like pancake mix and pasta sauce.

SHINSEGAE DEPARTMENT STORE

Map 1; 63 Sogong-ro, Jung-gu; ///radar.tangible.grit; www.woorisoolbang.com

At your next dinner party, skip the wine and impress your hosts with a bottle of fine Korean alcohol from Woorisoolbang, a beloved brand found in this classy department store. Crowd-pleasers include sugary *bokbunja-ju* (Korean blackberry wine) and *songi-ju* (rice wine flavored with pine mushrooms), but gifting a bottle of *insam-ju* (ginseng liquor) will guarantee a repeat invitation.

BEAUTIFUL TEA MUSEUM

Map 1; 19-11 Insadong-gil, Jongno-gu; ///tend.classic.sedated; 02-735-6678

Surely there's no better way to regale your friends with stories of your trip to Seoul than over a steaming cup of tea. Part shop, part museum, and part teahouse, the Beautiful Tea Museum is the place to pick up supplies, including over 100 types of tea and elegant porcelain cups to serve it in. Chosen your wares? Spend some time in the museum learning about Korea's tea culture and history, knowledge surely best shared over that next cuppa.

YEONNAM BANGAGAN

Map 3; 34 Donggyo-ro 29-gil, Mapo-gu; ///gangway.zone.ripe;
www.yeonnambangagan.com

Bangagan (mills) used to be neighborhood staples, where locals would bring sesame seeds or rice to be turned into oil or powder. They've largely been displaced by supermarkets, but Yeonnam Bangagan tries to keep that artisanal touch alive. It might not press everything in-house, but all of its products – from sesame oil to chocolate – have been made by Korean artisans.

NAMDAEMUN MARKET

Map 1; 3 Namdaemunsijang 4-gil, Jung-gu; ///answers.icon.started;
www.namdaemunmarket.co.kr

There's a saying in Seoul that "Namdaemun has everything except cat horns," testament to the market's 10,000 stores and hundreds, if not thousands, of products within each of them. There's plenty to browse, then, but seek out stainless steel chopsticks and kitchen scissors (often used in Korea instead of knives) for your cutlery drawers back home.

NOTDAM

Map 5; 729 Seolleung-ro, Gangnam-gu; ///social.strength.motor;
www.notdam.com

Koreans have been producing brassware for hundreds of years, with *bangjja* (high-quality brass tableware) a common feature on the tables of the royal family. Since 1993, the main company carrying on this tradition has been Notdam, whose creations are used in Seoul's Michelin-starred restaurants and five-star hotels – and in homes around the country, too. Pick up spoon and chopsticks sets along with stylish cutlery rests, or if the room in your suitcase allows, splash out on a noodle bowl or bulgogi grill.

» **Don't leave without** trying the face and skin massagers. As well as tableware, Notdam also makes tools for *gwalsa*, an East Asian style of massage that involves scraping the skin to stimulate blood flow.

SSG FOOD MARKET
Map 5; 442 Dosan-daero, Gangnam-gu; ///soda.parrot.slang; 02-6947-1286

This gourmet supermarket-meets-food hall is Shinsegae department store's foray into the high-end grocery business. It mainly serves the well-off families of southeast Seoul, who call in when the occasion warrants to pick up the likes of fresh mackerel and cooked meats. SSG is just as hot on dry goods and sauces, though, so splurge on high-quality pine nuts, rice powder, and a jar of gochujang.

Try it!
WRAP YOUR WARES

Bojagi – wrapping cloth – has made giving gifts an art form in Korea. Learn how to turn a piece of fabric into an elegant package, and how to tie your sack for good fortune, at Fold and Tie *(www.fold-tie.com)*.

Local Artisans

For such a trend-focused city, there's a huge amount of love and respect for traditional trades. Here, artisans have been chipping away at crafts like embroidery and shoemaking for decades.

TODOK WORKSHOP

Map 1; 60 Insadong-gil, Jongno-gu; ///speared.bleat.tripled; 0507-1383-3812

Koreans have long used name seals to sign documents, and these personalized stamps still hold up in a world that's mostly moved online. It's down to places like Todok, a name seal store and workshop that creates beautifully carved stone slabs. Buy a stamp pre-decorated with Seoul landmarks, or have your name engraved in Korean in around 20 minutes.

HEO SARANG

Map 2; 41-3 Shinheung-ro 2-ga, Yongsan-gu; ///bags.swim.jetted; www.heosarang.kr

If there's any indication of what *hanbok* – traditional dress – means to Korea, it's the government-designated National Hanbok Day (October 21, FYI). Locals don't wait until then to wear theirs, though.

Contact the owner in advance to book a fitting or check what sizes are available, since stock goes fast.

Not when Heo Sarang is bringing this Joseon-era item into the 21st century with funky designs (like kitsch tiger prints), shorter hems, and tighter fits.

SONSHINBAL

Map 3; 2 Yeonhui-ro 2-angil, Seodaemun-gu;
///marriage.passage.recovery; www.sonshinbal-shop.com

Branded sneakers might dominate the streets of Seoul, but Sonshinbal is almost single-handedly reviving the art of the handmade shoe – a trade that has been declining since its 1960s golden years. Okay, Sonshinbal's popularity has a lot to do with BTS, who wore the genderless shoes in their "Butter" music video, but it's also down to the high quality of the stock, whether it's white leather boots with chains, classic loafers, or thick-soled sandals.

SSAMZIGIL CENTER

Map 1; 44 Insadong-gil, Jongno-gu; ///beards.mascots.result;
02-736-0088

Ancient crafts might be the backbone of Seoul's art world, but there's a thriving contemporary artisanal scene that gets just as much respect. Take this five-floor shopping center, which breathes new life into the craft hub of Insadong with shops selling everything from new takes on embroidery to cat-themed stationery.

» Don't leave without exploring the workshops on the basement floor to learn how to weave, knit, and paint from experts.

Liked by the locals

"Society has changed dramatically, but one thing has withstood the test of time: art remains. No matter how our societies flux, or in what way we progress, there is always more room for art."

BYUNG-SUN BANG, PROFESSOR OF ART AND
ARCHAEOLOGY AT KOREA UNIVERSITY

OBJECT

**Map 3; 13 Wausan-ro 35-gil, Mapo-gu; ///disclose.sigh.goals;
www.insideobject.com**

Into journaling? This tiny stationery store is for you, though be warned.
You'll go in to pick up a notebook and leave with cute animal figurines
for your desk, a funky tumbler for your coffee, and a seashell lamp to
light up your writing sessions. It'll all be made by a local designer, too,
either up and coming or part of a beloved studio like Zero Per Zero.

HANSAEM LEATHER CRAFT WORKSHOP

**Map 3; 113 Eoulmadang-ro, Mapo-gu; ///possibly.rashers.crazy;
02-334-8427**

A fancy passport case is just as much a form of self-expression as new
sneakers in Seoul, and it's always worth paying for something long-
lasting. Pick a leather case from this workshop (throw in a wallet too),
and be assured it'll weather any storm on your life's travels.

» Don't leave without taking a class, where expert craftspeople will
teach you how to make single-fold wallets or friendship bracelets.

KOREA HOUSE

**Map 4; 10 Toegye-ro 36-gil, Jung-gu; ///still.fall.display;
www.chf.or.kr/kh**

Souvenirs get a tacky, touristy rep, but those sold at this theater gift
store aren't your average production-line products. Rather, calligraphy
sets, elegant lacquerware, and porcelain teapots are stamped by
Korea's most celebrated designers for a perfect gift.

Music Stores

K-pop might hog the headlines, but Seoulites are just as partial to a groovy guitar riff or emotional ballad. Happily, stores cater to all tastes, whether you're building a record collection or stocking up on merch.

NULLPAN

Map 3; 178-8 Yanghwa-ro, Mapo-gu; ///modes.powder.prefix; 10-6678-0213

For every K-pop tune, there's a rock alternative – and a small basement bar/record store from which to enjoy said alternative. NullPan is where like-minded people (read: those who reject bubblegum sounds) discuss Black Sabbath's greatest hits over a beer and thumb through new Korean rock records. Ask nicely, and the staff will play your chosen LP on the professional sound system.

WELCOME RECORDS

Map 2; 63 Sinheung-ro, Yongsan-gu; ///unto.whistle.spots; www.welcomerecords.kr

Welcome Records takes its name seriously by establishing a community of music lovers. It starts with the store's vibey atmosphere, where friends sip coffee in the café to a soundtrack of funk. It continues on the shop floor, where EDM, house, and hip-hop LPs aim to introduce beginners to record culture. And it culminates at the record release parties and DJ nights, where everyone is welcome to pop by, and many come wearing the store's oversized t-shirts.

KTOWN4U

Map 5; 513 Yeongdong-daero, Gangnam-gu; ///lighter.dime.arrived; www.ktown4u.com

Whether they're waved in unison during heartbreaking ballads or fluttered like pom-poms during a wild dance number, lightsticks are a constant at K-pop concerts across Korea. Every band has their own uniquely designed lightstick, and KTown4U is where to pick up those associated with groups from The Boyz to LOONA. Why not buy a BTS photocard pack, too, while you're at it?

MUSIC KOREA

Map 1; 3rd floor, 52 Myeongdong 8-gil, Jung-gu; ///crimson.beaters.parting; www.musickorea.com

One way to show your love for your favorite K-pop band? Wear all their merch and purchase all their music multiple times. This huge K-pop merchandise store helps you do both of these things, so stock up on official posters and branded t-shirts – perfect for bringing to fansign events that are often held here.

» Don't leave without checking out the K-drama merch, which includes *Squid Game* keychains, plushies of your favorite romantic characters, and original soundtrack CDs.

VINYL & PLASTIC

**Map 2; 248 Itaewon-ro, Yongsan-gu; ///grudges.walkway.stubbed;
www.dive.hyundaicard.com**

Having a Hyundai Card gets you places in Seoul – literally, only credit
card holders can access the Hyundai Card company's cultural spaces,
like its music library lined with 10,000 records. So when Hyundai
Card's first store, Vinyl & Plastic, opened its doors in 2022 to everyone, non-card holders were overjoyed. Collectors make the most of
the free rein here, browsing up to 4,000 LPs and 8,000 CDs, enjoying
a brew in the coffee shop, and sampling stacks of all genres in the
listening zone. Treating yourself? All credit cards are accepted.

» Don't leave without heading downstairs to the gallery space,
Storage, for exhibitions that span contemporary art, design, and film.

BEAT ROAD

**Map 3; 107 Donggyo-ro, Mapo-gu; ///brighter.shower.ribs;
www.beatroad.co.kr**

Let's face it: most people come to Seoul as a result of their undying
love for K-pop, which has seemingly reached every country on
earth. K-pop fans are a force to be reckoned with, whether they're
attending every BLACKPINK concert or buying advertising space
to celebrate BTS's anniversary. The Beat Road store facilitates the
connection between fans and idols – stars give back with frequent
fansign events and small live performances in-store, while fans show
their appreciation by renting out the shop for events that honor their
favorite groups and solo artists, like an idol's birthday or a band's
album release. Aside from all of this, Beat Road is fundamentally a

place to stock up on albums, expand your band memorabilia collection, and flick through photo books (and connect with other K-pop obsessives to find out where BTS go to eat).

HOEHYEON UNDERGROUND MARKET
Map 1; Chungmuro 1(il)-ga, Jung-gu; ///climbing.elbowed.blog
There's nothing dark and dingy about this subterranean spot. Korea's underground markets – often located above a subway station – tend to be the city's best shopping spots, and Hoehyeon is one of Seoul's finest. Back in the 1980s, it was the best place to find LPs, and despite the number of shops dwindling since then (no thanks to the rise of music technology), it remains a haven for serious collectors to go crate digging. Prices can be high but aren't unreasonable, considering the rarity and quality of most of the vinyls, which range from 1980s Korean pop to 1960s classical opera.

Hyundai Seoul *(108 Yeoui-daero, Yeongdeungpogu)* might seem like just another of Seoul's many malls, but it's the pop-up stores that make it stand out. Those with their finger on the pulse keep track of the mall's social pages, waiting for the announcement of the next pop-up. The stores are often a response to the latest trends in K-culture, and have included ones selling boy band Stray Kids' exclusive merchandise and celebrating the debut of girl group NewJeans.

An afternoon shopping along
Insadong-gil

Seoulites love a glitzy mall, but they still hold a special place in their hearts for their city's traditional shopping districts. The Insadong neighborhood has been a local hub since way back — we're talking early Joseon dynasty, when the government set up a training center for royal artists here. Today its main street, Insadong-gil, is home to dozens of art galleries, antique shops, teahouses, and indie stores selling traditional crafts alongside the latest gadgets. Visit on the weekend to see it come alive with snack vendors and performers.

1. Tongmungwan
55-1 Insadong-gil, Jongno-gu;
www.tongmunkwan.co.kr
///spacing.cobras.listings

2. Talbang
48 Insadong-gil, Jongno-gu;
www.talbang.modoo.at
///truck.date.smoker

3. Ssamzigil
44 Insadong-gil, Jongno-gu;
www.smartstore.naver.com/
ssamzigil
///beards.mascots.result

4. Kukje Embroidery
41 Insadong-gil, Jongno-gu;
www.kjasuwon.com
///pumps.falls.pointed

5. Beautiful Tea Museum
19-11 Insadong-gil, Jongno-gu;
02-735-6678
///tend.classic.sedated

Napcheong Bronzewear
///dragons.insert.youth

YULGOK-RO

JONGNO-DONG

YULGOK-RO 4-GIL

SAMBONG-RO

SAMCHEONG-
DONG

YULGOK-RO

0 meters 100
0 yards 100

SAMIL-DAERO

Scan the shelves at
TONGMUNGWAN
Seoul's oldest bookstore has
been trading in old and rare
books since 1934. Look out
for the family histories and
200-year-old tomes printed
using traditional woodblocks.

Find a mask at
TALBANG
Masked dances are a huge
part of Korea's folk culture,
and Talbang has been
making wooden masks of
well-loved characters for
more than four decades.

UIJEONGGUK-RO

INSADONG-GIL

1

2

Pick up some crafts at
KUKJE EMBROIDERY
Swing by this colorful shop to browse
coasters, pillows, socks, and artworks
by the city's finest textile artisans.

Browse indie boutiques at
SSAMZIGIL
This open-air mall is a contemporary
take on the Insadong shopping
experience, with dozens of boutiques
selling whimsical home goods.

3

4

SAMIL-DAERO

INSADONG-GIL

JONGNO-
DONG

**Napcheong
Bronzeware** *is one of
the best places in Seoul
to purchase bangjja,
opulent brass tableware
fit for Korean royalty.*

UIJEONGGUK-RO

INSADONG-5-GIL

INSADONG-5-GIL

5

JONGNO-
GU

Sip while you shop at
BEAUTIFUL TEA MUSEUM
Learn about the history and culture
of tea in Korea, linger over a warm
cup under the gorgeous skylight,
and treat yourself to an elegant
tea set by a local ceramist.

ARTS & CULTURE

Ancient theater traditions, cutting-edge architecture, and a popular culture scene that's taken over the world: there are so many reasons to celebrate this city and its arts.

City History

To understand modern Seoul you must first get to grips with its history – a story of colonization, war, and rapid industrialization that speaks to the resilience and creativity of Seoulites.

AMSA-DONG PREHISTORIC SETTLEMENT SITE

Map 6; 158 Godeok-ro, Gangdong-gu; ///hangs.compiled.awoken
www.sunsa.gangdong.go.kr

Seoul was largely rebuilt in the 20th century after the Korean War, so the fact that this Neolithic settlement site still exists is pretty incredible. Discovered in 1925, it's home to restored pithouses, an excavated pavilion, and a museum that offers insight into how prehistoric people here lived.

SEODAEMUN PRISON HISTORY HALL

Map 4; 251 Tongil-ro, Seodaemun-gu; ///layered.shows.loss;
www.sphh.sscmc.or.kr

When the Japanese authorities built this prison in 1908, it was meant to hold 500 prisoners. Just 11 years later it held 3,000, most of whom were pro-democracy activists. A symbol of the suffering that Koreans faced at the hands of their colonizers, this museum makes for a solemn visit, with exhibits detailing how prisoners were tortured and a memorial hall of photos of those who died here. Take a breather in the park, where monuments commemorate independence activists.

SEOUL MUSEUM OF HISTORY

Map 1; 55 Saemunan-ro, Jongno-gu; ///dust.cactus.salt; www.museum.seoul.go.kr

Did you know that trams ran in Seoul in the 1930s? That it has four UNESCO World Heritage Sites? Or that the Seoul metropolitan area is home to half of Korea's population? For fun facts and more, visit this museum, where urbanization models and photos detail the city's epic evolution, from prehistory to what's in store for the future (spoiler: a lot).

>> **Don't leave without** following the path behind the museum to Gyeonghuigung Palace, supposedly the most haunted site in Korea, visited by the ghost of the country's only Empress, Queen Min.

THE KING'S ROAD

Map 1; 21-18 Jeongdong-gil, Jung-gu; ///pleasing.young.later

This street tells a story like no other in Seoul. In 1896, months after the murder of Empress Min by sympathizers to the Japanese government, Emperor Gojong was forced to flee along this trail – dressed in women's attire – to seek asylum at the Russian Legation. This fateful morning still plagues many Koreans, who see Gojong's actions as the reason for Korea's fall to Japan; for others, walking the road is a time to reflect and ask, "well, what would I have done?".

BONGEUNSA TEMPLE

Map 5; 531, Bongeunsa-ro, Gangnam-gu; ///flat.cloth.ruffle;
www.bongeunsa.org

Buddhism hasn't always had an easy ride in Korea, and nor has this temple – the oldest in Seoul. Since 794, it's been through renamings, reconstructions, and relocations, not to mention the threat of the Joseon dynasty's neo-Confucian government, who oppressed Buddhism and relegated temples to mountain valleys. But with the help of Queen Munjeong in the mid-16th century, the religion was revived, and Bongeunsa remained in the heart of Seoul and become the primary Korean Buddhist Seon temple. Today, many locals come to stand in awe under the huge statue of Maitreya (the Future Buddha), one of the tallest stone statues in Korea.

» Don't leave without catching a percussion ceremony, performed by monks, at 4:10am or 6:40pm. It's meant to awaken all beings.

SM ENTERTAINMENT SEOUL FOREST

Map 5; 83-21 Wangsimni-ro, Seongdong-gu; ///files.liberty.talents;
www.smtown.com

It cannot be overstated how much K-pop has done for Korea, and how much SM Entertainment has done for K-pop. Founded in 1995, this Seoul-born agency was the first to start churning out stars like H.O.T, the first "idol group" to sell one million albums in Korea, and Girls' Generation, the first to be signed by a US label. SM has gone on to create countless stars, and the work never stops at its sleek new headquarters in Seoul Forest, which acts as an office space for SM employees, a rehearsal studio for idols, and a visitor center for fans.

Explore the influential SM universe by picking up exclusive merch, customizing prints of your favorite SM star, and entering the metaverse "Kwangya," where AI versions of idols live.

SEOUL URBAN LIFE MUSEUM
Map 6; 27 Dongil-ro 174-gil, Nowon-gu; ///compounds.terribly.includes; www.museum.seoul.go.kr

A Seoulite's personal history isn't tied up in epic battles that happened 5,000 years ago – it's reflected in their childhood toys, old apartments, and wedding dresses. This museum shares the history of the city's masses, examining how lives have changed since the 1950s through items donated by, or bought from, citizens. Long-timers get nostalgic over old noodle packaging while younger locals pore over old photos and explore recreations of late-20th century houses. It's an unfiltered insight into the stories of those around you.

Shh!

Look at a list of royal residences in Seoul and you're unlikely to find the relatively diminutive Unhyeongung Palace *(www.unhyeongung.or.kr)*. Made up of only three buildings, the palace grounds were home to royalty in the late Joseon era. Learn about the power-hungry father of Korea's first emperor through the attached museum, and stroll through the beautiful gardens in the warmer months.

Top Museums

The best thing about Seoul is its ability to look fearlessly into the future without forgetting its past – much like its museums. Here, thought-provoking collections cover everything from the alphabet to AI.

NATIONAL MUSEUM OF KOREAN CONTEMPORARY HISTORY

Map 1; 198 Sejong-daero, Jongno-gu; ///stew.pipes.tables; www.much.go.kr

Perhaps no century has impacted Korea as much as the 20th, which witnessed Japanese colonization, civil war, and the rise of Hallyu. This museum, dedicated to modern history, has locals feeling pretty proud of how far they've come as they listen to testimonies from the Korean War and learn about lesser-known independence activists.

T.UM

Map 1; 65 Eulji-ro, Jung-gu; ///snaps.nervy.remake; www.tum.sktelecom.com

It's a museum about the telecommunications giant SK Telecom, so yes, T.um is part corporate PR, part techno-saviorism. But hey, the company has some impressive accomplishments and ambitions to show off, including artificial intelligence, autonomous navigation, and hologram communications. Book onto a tour and you'll journey from a space control center to the "future city" of HI-Land, where the possibilities are genuinely exciting.

NATIONAL HANGEUL MUSEUM

Map 4; 139 Seobinggo-ro, Yongsan-gu; ///fancied.catching.laptop; www.hangeul.go.kr

Not many countries have a museum dedicated to their alphabet, but not many have an alphabet like Hangeul. Korean was once written in Chinese characters, but in 1443, King Sejong ordered a new system to reflect the uniqueness of the language – and that's exactly what this museum promotes. Whether you're uncovering Hangeul's philosophical inspirations or its place in K-pop, it'll inspire you to learn the language (if only to re-watch *Squid Game* without the subtitles).

SEOUL MUSEUM OF CRAFT ART

Map 1; 4 Yulgok-ro 3-gil, Jongno-gu; ///truly.deck.floating; www.craftmuseum.seoul.go.kr

So loved are Korea's artisans that many are hailed "Living National Treasures" for keeping ancient crafts like ceramics and folk painting alive. But Korea is also home to contemporary crafters modernizing these traditions. This museum honors both sides of the craft coin, housing some 23,000 works of art ranging from textiles to metal.

» Don't leave without finding the museum's 400-year-old gingko tree. Its leaves turn to a vibrant yellow in the fall.

Solo, Pair, Crowd

Got a day to yourself? Seeking a cultured afternoon with pals? Seoul has a museum to suit.

FLYING SOLO
A moment to reflect

Seeking some quiet contemplation in the hectic city? Visit the War Memorial of Korea near Itaewon, which commemorates the victims of Korea's many conflicts and provides an in-depth look at martial history.

IN A PAIR
Royalty for a day

Walk in the shoes of kings and queens at the National Palace Museum of Korea in Jongno. Challenge your mate to see who can find Jang Yeong-Sil's Self-Striking Water Clock first among 40,000 royal items.

FOR A CROWD
Get crafting

Learn about the master artist Han Sang-soo at the Hansangsoo Embroidery Museum, where you can take an embroidery class with your friends before hitting the exhibition halls.

THE WAR AND WOMEN'S HUMAN RIGHTS MUSEUM

Map 3; 20 World Cup buk-ro 11-gil, Mapo-gu;

///junior.enormous.restless; www.womenandwarmuseum.net

Japanese occupation in the early 20th century was a hard-hitting era in Korean history, with Japan exploiting the country's people and stifling identity. An especially painful part of colonialism was the sexual enslavement of thousands of women, who were under subjugation to Japanese troops during World War II. Some survivors started speaking out in the 1990s, and this moving museum raises awareness of their stories with first-person testimonies and poignant art. The demand for justice is still ongoing, with protests taking place outside the Japanese embassy every Wednesday since 1992.

SEOUL K-MEDI CENTER

Map 6; 26 Yangnyeongjungang-ro, Dongdaemun-gu;

///suddenly.stuffing.narrow; www.kmedi.ddm.go.kr

The scent of fresh herbs is the first sign that you're in Yangnyeong Market, where Seoulites shop for natural remedies to cure any and every ailment. Holistic medicines have been used here for centuries, and the K-Medi Center – located within this therapeutic heart of Seoul – promotes the long history of traditional Korean medicine. This three-floored space is home to a foot bath and herbal food dining hall, but it's the history museum that has the answers to whether dried persimmons or ginseng will best help your cold.

» Don't leave without visiting the K-Beauty Shop, where items are made out of traditional herbs and environmentally friendly ingredients.

Performing Arts

The city's performing arts scene is multifaceted, championing both traditional tales and global influences. Whether they're putting on ancient opera or avant-garde theater, the people of Seoul have soul.

NATIONAL GUGAK CENTER

Map 6; 2364 Nambusunhwan-ro, Seocho-gu;
///libraries.leaflet.grand; www.gugak.go.kr

Before K-pop there was *gugak*, a traditional form of music equally adored in the big city. Seoul's primary institution for *gugak*, this center was founded in 1951 with a mission to preserve and promote local sounds, many of which were stifled under Japanese occupation. Can't decide whether to attend a *pansori* (traditional opera with a

Try it!
DANCE, DANCE, DANCE

Being a K-pop star isn't easy, as you'll find out at the Real K-pop Dance Studio *(www. realkpopdance.com)*. Follow the lead of K-pop background dancers and learn a synchronized routine.

small cast), *aak* (royal court music), or farmers' music show? Do as the locals do and buy a Saturday Gugak Concert ticket, and experience the most beloved *gugak* genres in a series of epic performances.

ARKO ARTS THEATER
**Map 4; 7 Daehak-ro 8-gil, Jongno-gu; ///pure.stressed.clay;
www.theater.arko.or.kr**

State-funded by the National Arts Council of Korea, Arko gives younger, emerging artists a stage to perform their works – something they wouldn't have access to at larger, private venues. As a result, pieces can be experimental and free of restraint: past works include *All The Sex I've Ever Had*, a multilingual play about seniors' sex lives, and *The Story of Island*, reflections on the Jeju uprising of 1948 told through the bereaved families of the victims. English subtitles are only available for select productions and times, so check ahead.

SEJONG CENTER FOR PERFORMING ARTS
**Map 1; 175 Sejong-daero, Jongno-gu; ///motel.snipe.awoken;
www.sejongpac.or.kr**

In the same way that a bar has its regulars, Sejong has its patrons: the performing arts lovers who never fail to catch the latest theater, dance, or classical music show held here. It's the big hitter of Seoul's performance scene, and it's *big*, with various spaces – like the ornate Opera Theater and the cozy Chamber Hall – for its various shows.

» Don't leave without checking out the exhibition hall devoted to King Sejong, the creator of Hangeul script, on the B2 level.

NATIONAL THEATER OF KOREA

Map 4; 59 Jangchungdan-ro, Jung-gu;
///sweeper.removed.downhill; www.ntok.go.kr

This is the big one, home to not one, but *three* of Korea's major performance companies: the National Orchestra of Korea, the National Dance Company of Korea, and the National Changgeuk Company of Korea. So, you can expect world-class shows that span everything from traditional dance and opera (that's *changgeuk* in Korean) to contemporary plays and beloved musicals.

JEONGDONG THEATRE

Map 1; 43 Jeongdong-gil, Jung-gu; ///good.energetic.extreme;
www.jeongdong.or.kr

Even as new stories and global exports enter Seoul's theater world, Jeongdong keeps Korean history at its heart. Whether it's a play based on the life of a heroic Korean figure or a dance piece highlighting the lifestyles of *gisaeng* (female entertainers of the Joseon dynasty), tradition and folklore remain center stage.

MYEONGDONG NANTA THEATRE

Map 1; 26 Myeongdong-gil, Jung-gu;
///remote.expires.bucket; www.nanta.co.kr

The origins of Korean theater have their roots in *talchum*: traditional mask dance dramas performed by the working classes, who used physical comedy to mock the upper classes. *Talchum* endures today, and inspired the makings of *Nanta*, a musical performance featuring sounds made only with kitchenware. Expect high energy and gasps and belly laughs aplenty as three cooks fulfil a manager's seemingly impossible orders – to huge comedic effect.

LG ARTS CENTER

Map 6; 136 Joongang-ro, Gangseo-gu; ///river.improve.bags; www.lgart.com

It's owned by LG, so rest assured you'll get state-of-the-art sound, lighting, and staging here. You'll also get internationally renowned performances from the likes of contemporary dance choreographer Pina Bausch or the American jazz musician Pat Metheny. Don your best dress and impress your guest with a night at the ballet.

BLUE SQUARE

Map 2; 294 Itaewon-ro, Yongsan-gu; ///example.carpets.output; www.bluesquare.kr

Remember those global exports we mentioned? You'll find them at Blue Square, which opened in 2011 to foster Seoulites' ongoing passion for a global art scene. It's the largest performing arts hall in Korea, so it's only right that internationally acclaimed musicals such as *Jekyll and Hyde*, *Phantom of the Opera*, and *Mamma Mia!* are most often staged here (and tend to sell out instantly). Most of the performances are in Korean, but often feature English subtitles – not that you'll need them if you know ABBA's greatest hits.

» Don't leave without stopping by the upstairs bookstore and café, which stocks secondhand and newly published books.

Contemporary Architecture

The majority of Seoul's built environment is less than 50 years old, and a product of the rush to rebuild after the war. Look out for statement designs that boggle the mind and leave you inspired.

LIE SANGBONG HQ

Map 5; 451 Dosandae-ro, Gangnam-gu; ///notched.behind.jeep; www.liesangbong.com

When fashion designer Lie Sangbong was planning an HQ, he wanted a space that reflected the uniqueness of his line. A dramatic break from the symmetry of its neighbors, this slim building does just that, appearing cloud-like with ceramic panels clad in waves. Dreamy.

LOTTE WORLD TOWER

Map 6; 300 Olympic-ro, Songpa-gu; ///firmer.batches.mistaken; www.lwt.co.kr

At 1,820 ft (555 m), the Lotte corporation's skyscraper is Korea's tallest building (and the world's sixth). But that's not all it has to brag about. Inspired by ceramics, it was designed to resemble a calligraphy

Check out what Lotte has to offer inside, including its own mall, cinema, and Seoul Sky observatory.

brush, with pale glass and metal filigree accents. It's also environmentally friendly, and has wind power generators and a geothermal heating and cooling system.

KYUNGDONG PRESBYTERIAN CHURCH

Map 4; 204 Jangchungdan-ro, Jung-gu; ///safari.plans.ever; www.kdchurch.or.kr

Kim Swoo-geun, one of Korea's most revered architects, was the brains behind this redbrick structure, whose shape recalls both hands clasped in prayer and a medieval fortress. Kim designed the austere interior to resemble Roman catacombs, with the only natural light pouring in from a skylight and illuminating the cross above the altar.

» Don't leave without visiting during Sunday morning mass at 9:30 or 11:30am, when the lighting feels all the more heavenly.

EWHA CAMPUS COMPLEX

Map 4; 52 Ewhayeodae-gil, Seodaemun-gu; ///begin.villa.blessing; www.ewha.ac.kr

Just as inspiring as Ewha Womans University – Korea's first educational institution for women when it opened in 1886 – was the addition of this subtly descending walkway in 2008. The work of French architect Dominique Perrault, the uncanny corridor dips down past steel and glass walls; as you descend and then rise up the stairs, the growing and shrinking walls and the shifting sun and shadow blur indoors and out. It's disorienting, in a mesmerizing way.

KT&G SANGSANG MADANG

Map 3; 65 Eoulmadang-ro Mapo-gu, Hongdae; ///crest.dining.business; www.sangsangmadang.com

Everyone knows this cultural center as the "Why Butter Building," since the concrete pattern on its glazed exterior resembles both butter spreading on toast and the wings of a butterfly opening. Decide which side of the butter knife you're on, then head inside to check out the building's exhibitions and shops.

JONGNO TOWER

Map 1; 51 Jong-ro, Jongno-gu; ///shell.ahead.closets; 02-2198-2114

In the 1990s, halfway through building this new skyscraper, Samsung decided they didn't like the design, halted construction, and brought on the famed Uruguayan architect Rafael Viñoly to finish the job. Viñoly decided to split his structure into three: a convex 12-story

Mass Studies is one of Korea's top contemporary architecture firms, and its stunning buildings can be found throughout Seoul. In Yeouido, keep an eye out for the graceful S-Trenue Tower, which appears to comprise three buildings leaning against one another. Over in Gangnam, the pixelated Boutique Monaco seems to have had several chunks removed from its Lego-like facade, and in Bukchon, Songwon Art Center's low wedge looks like the prow of a ship.

lower section, a rectangular eight-story middle section, and a ring that floats above, supported by three tubes that house elevators. Marvel at the blue-green tower on a stroll through downtown Seoul.

DONGDAEMUN DESIGN PLAZA

Map 4; 281 Eulji-ro, Jung-gu; ///massing.smarter.records; www.ddp.or.kr

When it opened in 2014, this structure was like nothing else in Seoul. While traditional Korean architecture seeks to blend into its surroundings, the Zaha Hadid-designed building stood out: a curving, seemingly hovering model covered in 40,000 micro-perforated aluminum panels. It fast stirred up controversy for its "blinking spaceship" design and because the beloved Dongdaemun Stadium was demolished to make room for it, but that's all largely forgotten now, with attention directed towards the exhibitions and Seoul Fashion Week held inside.

» Don't leave without browsing the Dongdaemun Design Store, which stocks the likes of irreverent postcards made by Korean designers.

COEX STARFIELD LIBRARY

Map 5; 513 Yeongdong-daero, Gangnam-gu;
///hatter.cherish.empire; www.starfield.co.kr

Search #Seoul on social media and photos of this library dominate. Located in the COEX mall, it's not your average "could use some love" library; rather, it's a "look what a library can be!" book haven. Three huge wooden bookshelves house 50,000 underlit books, towering over visitors as they head up the escalators.

Art Galleries

There's a reason why the renowned Frieze Art Fair launched its first Asian fair in Seoul in 2022. The city embraces modern art and global names with fervor, resulting in a vibrant scene that's growing at speed.

LEEUM SAMSUNG MUSEUM OF ART

Map 2; 60-16 Itaewon-ro 55-gil, Yongsan-gu;

///reshape.caves.projects; www.leeum.org

Yes, it's owned by Samsung, but this gallery isn't an exercise in self-congratulation. Rather, the focus is on ancient and modern Korean art, with paintings and sculptures displayed across three buildings. (Okay, audio guides are powered by Samsung phones, but that's it.)

NAM JUNE PAIK ART CENTER

Map 6; 10 Baengnamjul-ro, Giheung-gu, Yongin-si;

///happily.wipe.dairies; www.njpart.ggcf.kr

Granted, this art center isn't *technically* in Seoul, but Nam June Paik has done so much for contemporary art that it's worth the short journey. The Seoul-born Korean American is known for many things: the founder of video art, coining the term "electronic superhighway" to describe the future of telecommunications, and dropping his

Southeast of central Seoul, the art center is an hour's metro ride from Myeong-dong Station.

pants when meeting US President Bill Clinton in 1998. All jokes aside, this center showcases his experimental works and those by others inspired by his media art.

THE NATIONAL MUSEUM OF MODERN AND CONTEMPORARY ART (MMCA)

Map 1; 30 Samcheong-ro, Sogyeok-dong, Jongno-gu;
///piglet.frizz.limit; www.mmca.go.kr

When the MMCA was established in Gwacheon in 1969, it did what no museum in Korea had done before: showcase both modern Korean and global art. It's since grown into four branches, but its Seoul site stands out for its extras, like a lecture hall where expert-led talks are held, and a film studio showing experimental art films.

» **Don't leave without** visiting the bookstore, which stocks tomes related to international contemporary artists as well as local names.

PIKNIC

Map 4; 30 Toegye-ro 6ga-gil, Jung-gu; ///hosts.lakes.purist;
www.piknic.kr

Piknic is more than a gallery – it's a clubhouse for the city's young professionals and vanguard-minded art critics. Visits often start with a ramble around the current exhibition, maybe installations promoting the value of gardens or lighting art themed around mindfulness. It's then onto the Scandi café to enjoy a coffee break and discuss the exhibition's merits.

SEOUL MUSEUM OF ART (SEMA)

Map 1; 61 Deoksugung-gil, Jung-gu; ///birds.joggers.lipstick;
www.sema.seoul.go.kr

SeMA is all about developing locals' interest in art. Learning is at the fore, with lecture halls and a library encouraging visitors to brush up on their Korean art knowledge, and exhibitions that spotlight female artists and global names like David Hockney.

THEATRE DES LUMIERES

Map 6; 177 Walkerhill-ro, Gwangjin-gu; ///hats.droplet.remover;
www.deslumieres.co.kr

You won't find static artwork in bulky frames here; rather, masterpieces are projected onto towering walls – only right in a city driven by tech. Immerse yourself in Yves Klein's infinite blues or Gustav Klimt's regal golds while transfixed by floating lights and music beats.

ARARIO MUSEUM

Map 1; 83 Yulgok-ro, Jongno-gu; ///often.clothed.snapping;
www.arariomuseum.org

The only thing quirkier than the modern art in this museum is how it's displayed. The labyrinthine building has seen installations by Nam June Paik tucked in maze-like corridors and paintings by Keith Haring hang under its low ceilings; part of the fun is navigating the narrow stairways to find the abstract pieces, which rotate often.

» Don't leave without having an experimental Korean lunch at Myomi, found in the glass building attached to the museum.

Liked by the locals

"The contemporary Korean art scene is at its most vibrant and vigorous ever, a result of Generation MZ's [Millenial and Gen Z] art fever."

MIA JUNG, HEAD OF ART TEAM AT ARTiPIO
ART COMMUNITY

A day obsessing over
all things Hallyu

If, like the rest of the world, you've been swept up by Hallyu (the Korean Wave), there's no better way to explore Seoul than through the lens of your most-loved K-pop and K-dramas. Shopping in the same boutique that dresses your favorite idols or finding the exact café where that screen couple you're shipping had their meet-cute can make your Seoul experience personal in a way that traditional museums just can't. And we're totally here for it. Indulge your obsessions and follow Korea's pop culture across the capital to wherever it may take you; just note that you'll need transportation between the tour's stops.

1. K-Star Road
///crisis.turkey.inflame

2. SM Entertainment
83-21 Wangsimni-ro, Seongdong-gu; www.smtown.com
///files.liberty.talents

3. Dalgona stand near Hyehwa Station
///tasty.rafters.words

4. HiKR Ground
40 Cheonggyecheon-ro, Jung-gu; www.hikr. visitkorea.or.kr
///tycoons.warriors.threaten

📍 **N Seoul Tower**
///jazzy.brand.revolts

📍 **Gangnam Style statue**
///angel.mocked.boss

Live the idol life at HiKR GROUND
Immerse yourself in Hallyu at this extended reality (XR) tech center. Make your own music video and find out where your top K-drama was filmed.

JONGNO-GU

④

SEOUL PLAZA

Towering above the capital from the summit of Namsan Mountain, N Seoul Tower is a regular scene-stealer in K-dramas and films.

YONGSAN GU

Dongjak Bridge

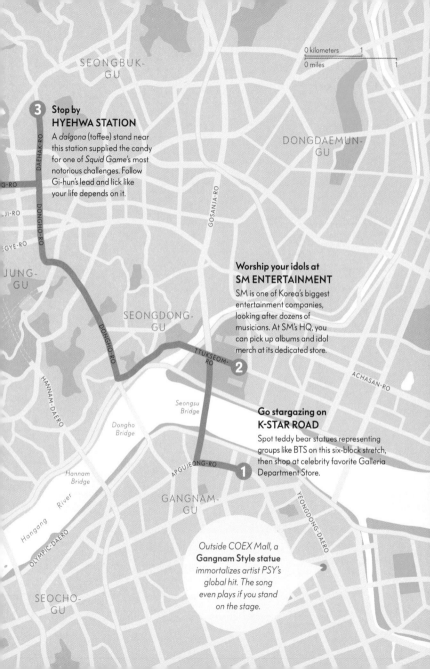

3 Stop by
HYEHWA STATION
A *dalgona* (toffee) stand near this station supplied the candy for one of *Squid Game*'s most notorious challenges. Follow Gi-hun's lead and lick like your life depends on it.

Worship your idols at
SM ENTERTAINMENT
SM is one of Korea's biggest entertainment companies, looking after dozens of musicians. At SM's HQ, you can pick up albums and idol merch at its dedicated store.

Go stargazing on
K-STAR ROAD
Spot teddy bear statues representing groups like BTS on this six-block stretch, then shop at celebrity favorite Galleria Department Store.

Outside COEX Mall, a **Gangnam Style statue** *immortalizes artist PSY's global hit. The song even plays if you stand on the stage.*

SEONGBUK-GU

DONGDAEMUN-GU

JUNG-GU

SEONGDONG-GU

GANGNAM-GU

SEOCHO-GU

DAEHAK-RO

DONGHO-RO

GOSANJA-RO

TTUKSEOM-RO

ACHASAN-RO

APGUJEONG-RO

YEONGDONG-DAERO

HANNAM-DAERO

OLYMPIC-DAERO

G-RO

JI-RO

EGYE-RO

DONGHO RO

Seongsu Bridge

Dongho Bridge

Hannam Bridge

Hangang River

0 kilometers   1
0 miles   1

NIGHTLIFE

Work (notoriously) hard, play harder – that's the Seoul way. As soon as the sun sets over the city, night-long marathons of eating, dancing, and singing ensue.

 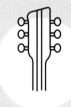 

Pochas and Convenience Stores

Any Seoul night out starts, continues, and ends with food. It's a rite of passage to congregate at **pochas** *(tent bars) and 24-hour convenience stores, filling up on street food while the good times roll.*

MAPO POCHA STREET

Map 4; Tojeong-ro 37-gil, Mapo-gu; ///basis.blacked.boomers

Conveniently situated in a large business district, this *pocha* street serves up some of Seoul's best street food to those needing a post-work feed. Every stall has bar-style seating, so do as the suited and booted do, *pocha*-hopping between stalls to try the likes of spicy udon, *tteokbokki*, and tempura.

EMART24 HANNAMDONG

Map 2; 245 Itaewon-ro, Yongsan-gu; ///tickets.grace.tickets; 02-798-0932

When you've had a long night out in Itaewon and need to refresh (or wait for a cab), this well-stocked Emart24 is a godsend. Hungry revelers heat up bulgogi boxes in the microwaves, and those winding down make a cup of tea with the hot water on tap. Yep,

Some convenience stores have lockers, so you can store your bags and coats while you go clubbing.

Seoul's convenience stores aren't your average kind – most come equipped with these amenities, plus seats on which to enjoy your buys.

EULJIRO NOGARI ALLEY

Map 1; Euljiro 13-gil, Jung-gu; ///hang.probable.retained; 02-2274-1040

So loved is this *pocha* alley that it's been designated a "Seoul Future Heritage" site to try to preserve it. It dates back to 1980, when a pub opened here serving *nogari* (dried pollack), popular with laborers working nearby. Half a century on, a number of restaurants have popped up alongside the pub, with *nogari* a menu mainstay. Pair your pollack with a shot of soju and you'll see why.

» Don't leave without trying the various types of dried fish served here, including codfish, which is perfect with a cold glass of beer.

HANSHIN POCHA SINCHON

Map 3; 1st floor, 10-4 Yonsei-ro, 7an-gil, Seodaemun-gu;
///tramps.primed.physics; 02-333-3284

It's helmed by celebrity chef Baek Jong-won, so Hansin isn't your average *pocha* – for one, tents and stalls are swapped out for an indoors restaurant. But, close your eyes, and the experience is no different, with the flavors you'd expect of typical *pocha* fare. Order the specialty: spicy chicken feet and *jumeokbap* (seasoned rice balls with dried seaweed), washed down with a sweet highball. It's a local favorite for its balance of spicy and nutty flavors.

DALMAEK SUPER

Map 2; 1st floor, 54 Noksapyeongdae-ro 7-gil, Yongsan-gu; ///went.ears.beards; 0507-1320-9963

This is one of those trendy stores that you don't want to say you're obsessed with, but you just are. Friends meet here for start-of-the-night drinks, grabbing a beer, cider, or wine from the fridges and cracking it open in the seating area. Drinking games unfold on some tables, catch-ups on another, before it's onto the next destination.

JONGNO 3-GA POCHA STREET

Map 1; 38 Donhwamun-ro 11-gil, Jongno-gu; ///gasping.exile.birds

This is as quintessential a *pocha* street as you can get, the tantalizing smell of grilled meat, seafood, and chicken wafting down the lively road. Pull up an iconic red or blue plastic stool, and enjoy spirited conversations over cheap beer.

» Don't leave without hopping between stalls to get a *tteokbokki* appetizer, fried chicken main, and *hotteok* (filled pancake) for dessert.

GS25 SEBITSEOM

Map 5; 2085-14 Olympic-daero, Seocho-gu; ///fuels.grazed.stored; www.gs25.gsretail.com

What makes this branch different from the countless other GS25 convenience stores in Seoul, you ask? Its location on the Sebit Isles, home to the best view of the Banpo Bridge Moonlight Rainbow Show every night. Pick up a *kimbap* and a beer inside, then find a spot on the grass along the river to watch water dance to light and music.

Liked by the locals

"A *pocha* is more than a tent restaurant – it's a place to blow off steam or satisfy late-night cravings. Whether it's a cold winter night or a humid summer evening, these glowing food stalls hold a special place in everyone's hearts, across all generations."

MIN JUNG KIM, PRODUCER AT *THE KOREA HERALD*

Game Night

Nightlife in Seoul is all about letting loose, but that's not limited to rowdy drinking dens and sweaty clubs. For those craving a release from reality or a quiet night with a board game, there's a place to hit the spot.

GOLFZON PARK

Map 5; 11 Samseong-ro 95-gil, Gangnam-gu;
///national.evolves.business; www.golfzonpark.com

A handful of Koreans are among the world's top female golfers, and when colleagues bustle into this screen golf spot after work, there's always one trying to become the next Pak Se-ri. For the rest, it's simply a fun night out – a chance to review their best swings on a golf simulator course in Hawaii or England, and bond with co-workers while chatting wind speeds. Golf shoes and gloves included.

SEOUL ESCAPE ROOM

Map 3; 11 Wausan-ro 17-gil, Mapo-gu;
///taster.starters.binders; www.seoul-escape.com

When K-dramas like *Squid Game* and *All of Us Are Dead* hinge on the fight for survival, it's little surprise that Seoulites get a kick out of escaping their own demise in 60 minutes. Seoul Escape Room was the first "exit game" site to open here in 2015, and remains the go-to spot for thrilling puzzle solving. Whichever themed room gets your adrenaline going (prove your innocence after being framed for murder, say, or break out of a haunted medieval mansion), reserve a spot for it online. Don't worry if you don't make it out within the hour; you will survive (your dignity might not, though.)

VR ZONE

**Map 4; 6th floor, iPark Mall, 17 Hangang-daero 21na-gil, Yongsan-gu;
///owns.stump.zipped; www.vrzone.modoo.at**

We all need a break from reality sometimes, and this virtual reality (VR) gaming den offers just that. Here, sports fanatics enjoy horse-back rides, dating duos ride rollercoasters, and mates go on jungle adventures – simply by wearing a VR headset. Welcome to the future.
» Don't leave without visiting the nearby CGV cinema to catch a movie to end your night, since VR Zone closes relatively early at 9pm.

LOTTE WORLD

**Map 6; 240 Olympic-ro, Songpa-gu; ///juggler.hesitate.amount;
www.lotteworld.com**

A year-round ice skating rink, a huge shopping mall, a fun-filled amusement park: there's enough going on at this recreation complex to spend a whole day here – and the night, too. Come in the evening, when lights are projected onto the theme park's so-called Magic Castle and fireworks shoot across the sky. Enjoy the colors while taking a scream-inducing plunge on Gyro Drop.

Solo, Pair, Crowd

Whether you're after a new hobby or you're all about (healthy) competition, there's a game night to suit.

FLYING SOLO

Get your skates on

Inspired by the roller skaters cruising along the Han River? Practice your own four-wheeled skills in the safety of Fantasy Boy Roller Club in Gangdong-gu, gliding to upbeat music until close at 10pm.

IN A PAIR

Amazing mazes

Not enough of you to do an escape room? Head to Dynamic Maze, an indoor obstacle course full of fun missions, a giant ball pit, and, of course, mazes. The spaces are all pretty tight — perfect for two people.

FOR A CROWD

Game on

Bring some friends and your competitive spirit to the Red Button Board Game Café in Gangnam, where drinks are plentiful and the selection of board games (like Clue, Avalon, and Rummikub) even more so.

PEAK PC BANG

Map 1; 33 Jong-ro, Jongno-gu; ///hardens.phones.dweller;
02-2158-6951

It's an understatement to call Seoulites big gamers – this is one of the world's most wired cities, where e-sports players are as loved as K-pop stars. For those who haven't made a career out of playing *League of Legends*, *PC bang* (literally PC rooms) are a place to hone gaming skills and escape into a fantasy world until the early hours – or 24/7, if you're visiting PeaK PC Bang. With state-of-the-art desktops, ergonomic chairs, and the ability to order food to your desk without interrupting flow, why would you game anywhere else?
>> Don't leave without ordering ramen for a boost of energy mid-game – eating junk food in a *PC bang* is all part of the experience.

SU NORAEBANG

Map 3; 67 Eoulmadang-ro, Mapo-gu; ///butter.hunches.giggle;
02-322-3111

It's not a Korean night out unless it ends at a *noraebang* – private singing rooms rented by the hour and decked out with huge screens and disco balls. (Note that some Koreans avoid using the word "karaoke," given the sensitivity around it being a Japanese term.) You'll find *noraebang* on every street corner in Seoul, but Hongdae's Su Noraebang is a crowd favorite for its expansive collection of international songs and translated lyrics. If you feel like putting on a show, ask for one of the rooms with floor-to-ceiling windows overlooking Hongdae Street – it feels like the room is your own personal stage, and Seoul your audience.

Cool Clubs

It's not just K-pop idols or B-boys who can bust a move – Seoulites love dancing the night away. Bring your A-game and some stamina: clubbing often continues until the subway restarts at 5:30am.

TIMES

Map 5; 25 Apgujeong-ro 54-gil, Gangnam-gu;
///december.commented.loaded

Apgujeong has made a name for itself on the underground clubbing scene in the last few years, thanks to new venues popping up in discreet corners. Times is arguably the flagship for this burgeoning scene, and has an air of exclusivity about it, but don't let that put you off: everyone's welcome to get down to the hip-hop and R&B mixes (including pop stars, who casually pop by to grab the mic).

MODECI

Map 3; 64 Wausan-ro, Mapo-gu; ///frocks.supper.spelled; 02-690-2285

It might be in the middle of a rowdy student neighborhood, but MODECi isn't your average raucous student club. Rather, it's a sophisticated hub for electronic music, providing a platform for small labels of different subgenres to showcase new sounds. It's a favorite place to play for long-time local heroes of the underground scene like Closet Yi, DJ Soulscape, and Co.Kr – keep an eye out for nights when they're behind the decks.

>> **Don't leave without** heading up to the second dance floor, which opens on the rooftop in the warmer months.

THE HENZ CLUB

Map 3; 64 Wausan-ro, Mapo-gu; ///frocks.supper.spelled

No, the identical address to MODECi is not a mistake – while these two clubs share the same building, they couldn't be more different. This basement club is a crucial link between the underground rap scene and hip-hop, which have been making waves in Seoul thanks to the rise in rap battle and B-boy dance competitions on TV. Nights here are often intense, where emerging rap talent cuts its teeth and DJs drop trap beats that'll have you popping B-boy-inspired moves.

JEOUL GALLERY

Map 2; 62 Bogwang-ro 59-gil, Yongsan-gu; ///rent.smoker.verge

There are no contact details for this gallery and club: only the notion that if you know, you know. Art students amble around the gallery in the day, returning at night for the DIY techno club, where DJs work the bar before getting behind the decks. Since it's tucked down a dark, residential alley, the police often come to shut it down due to noise complaints from residents. Stay cool – it's not an illegal club, and it doesn't take more than a few minutes before the music restarts (at a quieter volume, mind).

CAKESHOP

Map 2; 134 Itaewon-ro, Yongsan-gu; ///residual.cable.portable;
www.cakeshopseoul.com

Surviving Seoul's notoriously fickle trend landscape is no easy
feat for any business, but Cakeshop has managed to stay open —
and thrive — for over a decade. Its secret? Continuously challenging
its audience. Expecting a standard night of hip-hop, electronic,
and techno? DJs will throw in garage, disco, UK bass, reggaeton,
and alt-K-pop for good measure, all to keep you on your toes
(literally, dancing can get *sweaty* here). If you're picky, check
Cakeshop's social pages to find out what sound will dominate
the night; if you're not, let the world-class local and global DJs
take the lead.

≫ **Don't leave without** finding out when the next pop-up queer night,
Sins, is on; it's been instrumental in growing the city's LGBTQ+ culture,
and always promises a good time.

PAPER/SHELTER

Map 2; 5th floor, 37 Itaewon-ro 27ga-gil, Yongsan-gu;
///suitcase.clearly.dome

In the midst of Itaewon's packed nightlife streets, pushy promoters
and long lines give way to an oasis of class and cutting-edge
at this double-heading club — one of the newer additions to
Seoul's clubbing scene. While Paper offers sophisticated lounge
vibes for the city's suave crowds, Shelter (located just a staircase
above) offers a slight shift with its dark, energetic atmosphere
set to the tune of techno. Entry fees cover both clubs, so you can

roam freely between the two floors while taking in the irresistible panoramic skyline view as you go. Two clubs for the price of one? Count us in.

FAUST

Map 2; 7 Bogwang-ro 60-gil, Yongsan-gu; ///defend.haggle.earlobe; 70-7757-4789

On an exchange semester in Germany, music maker Marcus Lee explored the country's cavernous techno clubs and wondered why no such thing existed in Korea. Thought turned into action, and he decided to open a pocket of Berlin in Seoul; Faust has since risen to become Seoul's premier techno venue, satiating — and, dare we say, leading — the city's blossoming electronic subculture. It's delightfully no-frills, with attention focused on the epic sound system and the deep musical experience ravers have as a result.

The team behind Soap Seoul (www.soapseoul.com) is a huge player in Korea's underground music scene, but still manages to keep some things a secret until the last minute — like the annual rooftop party held on Seoul's Floating Islands in the summer. The event gathers the most notable DJs from the techno and hip-hop scene for an all-day party with two dance floors. Want in? Keep an eye on the group's social pages, and be ready to drop everything when the date's announced.

Music Nights

You're in Korea, so listening to K-pop – which we all know and love – is a given. But this city's music scene has so much more besides. Heavy metal, indie pop, smooth jazz: you'll hear them all here.

BOOGIE WOOGIE

Map 2; 21 Hoenamu-ro, Yongsan-gu; ///strapped.drama.shade; 010-2966-0209

Jazz made its way to Korea after World War II, when clubs began to cater to US soldiers stationed in Seoul. Since then, a small but diehard group of jazz lovers has continued growing, and Boogie Woogie is something of their insider clubhouse. For one, you must reserve a spot inside by texting the number listed – no calls. Once

Try it!
MAKE SOME MUSIC

Korean folk is one of the country's most respected music forms. Try playing some of the genre's pivotal instruments, like a *janggu* (hourglass drum) and a *gayageum* (zither), at the National Gugak Center *(p122)*.

inside, denizens groove to funky riffs coming from local and global artists who play nightly. There's no entrance fee, but the performances will (literally) sway you to leave a tip for the musicians; envelopes for your cash are provided by the staff along with your cocktail bill.

» Don't leave without heading one floor up to see what's playing at Pet Sounds, a separate venue known for retro and indie rock.

SEOUL COMMUNITY RADIO

Map 2; 22 Noksapyeong-daero 40na-gil, Yongsan-gu, Itaewon;
///written.kicked.such; 10-3091-9199

Seoul Community Radio (SCR) started life as an online radio broadcasting platform in 2016, livestreaming DJ sets in the hope of inspiring new talent. Four years later, SCR opened this intimate music studio and bar to take this mission to new heights, with live shows and workshops drawing creatives who come to mingle and experiment with sounds. It's a pretty casual hangout, like popping over to your mate's apartment for a laid-back evening of tunes.

CHANNEL 1969

Map 3; 35, Yeonhui-ro, Mapo-gu; ///quarrel.download.brochure

Seoul's alternative underbelly lives strong in this dark den, which manages to be a club, live music hall, and lounge all at once. Under reflecting disco lights, indie rock bands play soulful riffs, DJs spin psychedelic tunes, and noise musicians experiment with sounds. Between sets, everyone pours onto the street outside to chat, smoke, and cool down from the sweaty hotbox inside.

LA CLE

Map 4; 95-2 Samcheong-dong, Jongno-gu;
///cutaway.timidly.elevator; www.lacle.modoo.at

If anywhere proves that Seoul's got soul (sorry), it's this basement jazz bar. There's nothing fancy about it: in front of LP-lined bookcases is a makeshift stage, on which different groups strum their instruments beautifully from 8pm. To enter, there's a pretty low cover fee of 3,000 won, which is cash only.

SENGGI STUDIO

Map 3; 137 Wausan-ro, Mapo-gu; ///message.treaties.treating;
www.senggistudio.com

There's no other way to put it: Senggi Studio is just *cool*. It's primarily a recording studio, so every high note or bass tone coming through the top-quality speakers is as smooth as smooth can be. As for the music itself, expect experimental sounds from emerging underground artists. Check the website for show details.

GOPCHANG JEONGOL

Map 3; 8 Wausan-ro 29-gil, Mapo-gu; ///rates.hamster.quickly

Forget the Korean Wave – for Seoulites, it's all about the retro wave impacting everything from fashion to music. The decades between 1960 and the early 2000s saw huge growth within Korea, and even those who weren't there to witness it feel a certain nostalgia for the period. A product of this love for all things retro is the growth of LP bars like this one, where fashionably dressed-down locals make song requests while nursing a whiskey. It's chill for the most part, but sometimes, that one 1990s crowd favorite has everyone breaking into a sing-along.

» Don't leave without requesting a track on a slip of paper near the bar. As long as it's from no later than the early 2000s, it'll be welcome.

CHWIHAN JEBI

Map 3; 24 Wausan-ro, Mapo-gu; ///humble.thank.weekends; 02-325-1969

Walls lined with comic books, VHS tapes, and memorabilia from the 1980s and 90s: we told you this city loves its retro. So do the brothers who set up this indie rock venue – a café by day called Jebi Dabang, bar by night called Chwihan Jebi, and headquarters of a record label 24/7. To indicate the shift from day to night, staff slide a signboard over the word "Dabang" on the exterior, amusingly changing the name's meaning from "swallow café" to "drunken swallow". Do as the name suggests and order a drink before settling in for a show.

OLYMPIC HALL

Map 6; 424 Olympic-ro, Songpa-gu; ///infects.saints.staple; www.ksponco.or.kr/olympicpark

When it comes to K-pop, most roads lead to this huge venue. New group? They'll likely debut here in a "showcase," when they perform to fans for the first time (Treasure and EXO got their start here). Making a "comeback" with new music? It'll be performed here, like SEVENTEEN did with their mini album "Al1". As expected, tickets sell out at lightning speed, so keep your eye on the website.

LGBTQ+ Friendly

LGBTQ+ acceptance has been slow in Korea, and welcoming spaces are vital for the queer community. While many places work through word-of-mouth, here are some that openly identify as LGBTQ+.

SAEKDAREUN HANJAN

Map 3; 35 Dongmak-ro 2-gil, Mapo-gu; ///legend.positive.pancakes; 070-4222-4198

As the colorful poster by the door here asks, "Why be racist, sexist, homophobic, transphobic when you could just be quiet?". For the LGBTQ+ customers and allies who get together at this laid-back food spot, conversations are only ever joyful – as expected when there are cute pups to pet, new friends to make, and fried chicken to devour here.

HEY JUDE BAR

Map 3; 7 Wausan-ro 37-gil, Mapo-gu; ///mining.remote.bespoke; 10-4077-4851

Hey Jude is the kind of place to rock up to, and leave, early – but that's no bad thing. Practically speaking, the queer-owned bar reaches full capacity quickly, its cozy seats occupied by dates (and mates) enjoying hushed conversations over negronis and non-alcoholic cocktails. Doors close at 11pm, but hey, if the date's gone well, head onto round two – we recommend nearby Saekdareun Hanjan.

BAR GNOME

Map 1; 50-2 Supyo-ro 22-gil, Jongno-gu; ///crew.selects.stuffing

Anyone who's spent the evening at this spot raves about the same thing: the owner, who's as famously welcoming to tourists and newbies as he is to regulars. While the host whips up colorful cocktails in suggestive glasses (often of the phallic nature), he'll bring you into the conversations he's having with those sitting at the bar, offering English translations if needed. Add to that free condoms and lube and you've got yourself a bar that's yet to receive less than a five-star review.

» Don't leave without taking your cocktail up to the rooftop, which overlooks the city's government district.

BAR FRIENDS

**Map 4; 7 Supyo-ro 28-gil, Jongno-gu; ///wires.rope.bravery;
02-766-5334**

There's no false advertising here: this really is the place to make new friends or come arm-in-arm with those you already have. Rough day? Chat to the English-speaking staff while they pour you a wine (the specialty here). Hoping to find like-minded people? We guarantee there's a group happy to welcome you to their table.

Liked by the locals

"Seoul's queer scene is full
of vibrant, eccentric, and exciting
people. You can always find
something going on, whether it's
an art show, a drag show, or a
burlesque show. Come for the
shows, but stay for the people."

MAIA P. SPARKLES, DRAG PERFORMER

BOTTOMS UP

Map 2; 37 Usadan-ro, Yongsan-gu; ///rumbles.yourself.javelin; 50-5506-1212

Not everyone's fond of the name of Itaewon's "Homo Hill." Its other names, "The Hill" and "LGBTQ Street," are far more representative of this inclusive alleyway, home to a dozen LGBTQ+ venues where everyone is welcomed with open arms. Of all the bars, Bottoms Up is the place to see and be seen, its big windows perfect for you to watch the comings and goings of the street and eye up those who enter the bar's folds. Though the crowd (mostly men) all seem to know each other, newcomers are made to feel like part of the family, with closely knit tables encouraging intimate chats and dim lighting encouraging, well, maybe a little bit more.

RABBITHOLE ARCADE PUB

Map 2; 37 Sinheung-ro, Yongsan-gu; ///taker.prefer.secretly; 10-8259-2280

Rabbithole is not for the timid. It gets sticky, gritty, crowded, and noisy, but that's exactly why it's one of the hottest joints for Seoul's queer community. Aside from the hands-in-the-air boogying that happens here, it's the Friday and Saturday night drag shows that attract the most noise. Drag has long been shrouded in taboo (and thus is rare) in Korea, but if anywhere can be the source for change, it's Rabbithole, where many of the country's best burlesque and drag performers – including HoSo Terra Toma – have gotten their start.

» Don't leave without ordering a creative cocktail, themed around something like a Harry Potter house or Pokémon character.

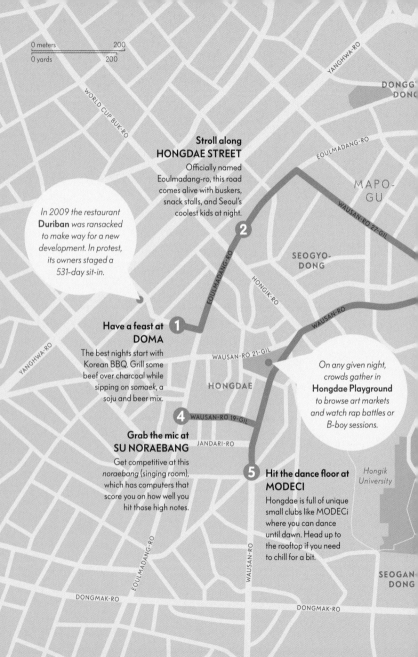

**Stroll along
HONGDAE STREET**
Officially named
Eoulmadang-ro, this road
comes alive with buskers,
snack stalls, and Seoul's
coolest kids at night.

2

*In 2009 the restaurant
Duriban was ransacked
to make way for a new
development. In protest,
its owners staged a
531-day sit-in.*

**Have a feast at
DOMA**
The best nights start with
Korean BBQ. Grill some
beef over charcoal while
sipping on *somaek*, a
soju and beer mix.

1

*On any given night,
crowds gather in
Hongdae Playground
to browse art markets
and watch rap battles or
B-boy sessions.*

4 WAUSAN-RO 19-GIL

HONGDAE

**Grab the mic at
SU NORAEBANG**
Get competitive at this
noraebang (singing room),
which has computers that
score you on how well you
hit those high notes.

5 **Hit the dance floor at
MODECI**
Hongdae is full of unique
small clubs like MODECi
where you can dance
until dawn. Head up to
the rooftop if you need
to chill for a bit.

*Hongik
University*

0 meters 200
0 yards 200

WORLD CUP BUK-RO

YANGHWA-RO

EOULMADANG-RO

MAPO-
GU

WAUSAN-RO 27-GIL

SEOGYO-
DONG

DONGG
DONG

EOULMADANG-RO

HONGIK-RO

WAUSAN-RO

WAUSAN-RO 21-GIL

YANGHWA-RO

JANDARI-RO

EOULMADANG-RO

WAUSAN-RO

DONGMAK-RO

DONGMAK-RO

SEOGAN
DONG

A classic night out in
Hongdae

Home to art studios and dim basement clubs, Hongdae rose to prominence in the 1990s as Seoul's center of alternative culture. Its popularity inevitably led to massive gentrification, but the area retains its indie streak, and it remains a favorite among the city's coolest crowds. And with tons of pubs and clubs that stay open until the sun comes up, Hongdae nights are still the stuff of legend. Party like the locals do in *cha* (or rounds), moving between venues while you eat, drink, and sing the night away. Stamina required.

3 **Catch a show at SENGGI STUDIO**
Buy tickets in advance, or chance your luck at the door, at this concert venue, arts space, and recording studio.

Wausan Mountain

SINCHON-RO

WAUSAN-RO 35-GIL

WAUSAN-RO

1. Doma
33 Yanghwa-ro-16-gil, Mapo-gu; 02-3143-0365
///eggs.disclose.twisting

2. Hongdae Street
///readings.fountain.sweeter

3. Senggi Studio
137 Wausan-ro, Mapo-gu;
www.senggistudio.com
///message.treaties.treating

4. Su Noraebang
67 Eoulmadang-ro, Mapo-gu; 02-322-3111
///butter.hunches.giggle

5. MODECi
64 Wausan-ro, Mapo-gu; 02-690-2285
///frocks.supper.spelled

Duriban
///deep.moon.elevate

Hongdae Playground
///keepers.discount.jaunts

OUTDOORS

Seoul might be Korea's urban epicenter, but with its temple-dotted mountains, elegant footpaths, and green parks, the city is perfect for alfresco adventures.

Scenic Strolls

*Vast green forests, mural-lined alleyways in
quaint villages, verdant parks with skyline views:
Seoul was made for a stroll. So lace up those
sneakers, there's a city to explore.*

SEOULLO 7017

Map 4; start at Seoul Station, Jung-gu; ///scramble.bowhead.winner

Nothing symbolizes Seoul's shift from traffic-choked concrete jungle
to walkable wonderland better than Seoullo. This elevated half-a-
mile (1-km) garden was laid out across a 1970s highway overpass in
2017 (hence the digits in its name), and has since become the go-to
spot for a dreamy walk to work or a weekend wander. Climb the steps
by Seoul Station to find lily pad-dotted ponds and over 24,000
plants laid out in artfully arranged flowerbeds. And, relax.

CHEONGGYECHEON

**Map 1; start at Cheonggye Plaza, Jongno-gu;
///clearing.learns.grandson**

Just like Seoullo, this was once a congested highway, before local
residents demanded more outside space for some much needed
R&R. Thanks to their collective efforts, a lush 7-mile (11-km) river was

restored in the road's place in 2005, cutting through the thriving heart of downtown Seoul. From Cheonggye Plaza, the route can be followed all the way down to the verdant banks of the Han River, where you'll find joggers, picnickers, and photo-snapping tourists.

» **Don't leave without** visiting the Palseokdam Pond near the river's start. The pond is made of stones sourced from Korea's eight provinces.

SEOKCHEON LAKE PARK

Map 6; start at Lotte Tower, Songpa-gu; ///skims.ranted.woes

Between March and mid-April, the social media feeds of almost every young Seoulite are suddenly awash with shades of pink. It can mean only one thing: it's cherry blossom season. During the beloved Seokcheon Lake Cherry Blossom Festival, the park's pastel-carpeted grounds, home to over 1,000 cherry trees, are the ideal spot for a saunter. Bypass the hordes and start your walk early, camera in hand – just don't forget to add the obligatory *beotkkot* (cherry blossom) hashtag to your socials.

SEOUL BOTANIC PARK

Map 6; start at Magoknaru Subway Station exit 3, Gangseo-gu;
///shaky.humidity.spoken; www.botanicpark.seoul.go.kr

Seoul might once have been known as the "grey city" due to its penchant for concrete, but planners now work tirelessly to shake off this rep. And green spaces like the Botanic Park are helping. For a small fee, join the throngs of families and school trips exploring the park's lush greenhouses, wetlands, and forests.

GYEONGBOKGUNG PALACE

Map 1; start at 61 Sajik-ro Jongno-gu; ///shell.vanish.unveils;
www.royalpalace.go.kr

It might be one of Seoul's most famous sights, but not even the swarms of tourists could deter locals from the so-called "palace greatly blessed by Heaven." And a walk through the grounds of this former royal residence is indeed heavenly, with opulent gates and pavilions backed by pine-covered mountains rising in the north.

YANGJAE CITIZEN'S FOREST

Map 6; start at Yanjae Citizens Forest Station, Seocho-gu;
///vertical.onions.amount; www.parks.seoul.go.kr

We could reel off some impressive stats about this forest: it stretches for over 90 acres (350,000 sq m), for example, and has over 95,000 trees of 43 different species. But numbers can't capture the magic

Shh!

Seoul's French population might be small, but they've certainly left their mark on Seorae Village, sometimes nicknamed Montmartre. Hidden well beyond the tourist trail in the Seocho district, here you can channel your inner *flâneur* or *flâneuse*, strolling past bottle shops purveying the finest French vintages, and quaint *boulangeries* peddling freshly baked baguettes. Swing by in September and there's even a small French-Korean music festival. *Très chic!*

of an autumnal walk under its canopy, as persimmons and quinces cascade from branches, and the auburn foliage seems to burn as it catches the light. Wrap up warm, and lose yourself in Yangjae.

GYEONGUI LINE BOOK STREET

Map 3; start at Hongik University Station, Mapo-gu;
///cubes.protests.patio; www.gbookst.or.kr

Nestled along the old railway line between Hongik University station and Sinchon lies a row of bookshops housed in old train cars, commemorating the 1,000-plus publishing companies once based in the area. Meander along the path in spring, when the persimmon trees are in bloom, and finish in one of the wine bars along the route.

» Don't leave without walking under the old bridge, decked out with framed prints of Korea's favorite book covers.

IHWA MURAL VILLAGE

Map 4; start at exit 2 of Hyehwa Station, Jongno-gu; ///tiger.skills.fronted

Ihwa was one of Seoul's many *daldongne*, or moon villages: poor neighborhoods built high on hillsides after the Korean War. It was rather overlooked until 2006, when the local government enlisted artists to splash its walls with a colorful assortment of flowers, robots, and angel wings, as well as a famed mural of a koi carp. Walking its kaleidoscopic streets is now a given when in Seoul, but the influx of noisy outsiders has vexed locals – so much so that the koi mural was painted over as an act of resistance. By all means come for a stroll, but be mindful of the locals as you do.

Picnic Spots

Seoul's love of convenience and plethora of lunch spots make picnicking truly special. With delivery scooters bringing hot meals anywhere, you've never picnicked quite like this before.

SEOUL FOREST

Map 5; 273 Ttukseom-ro, Seongdong-gu; ///asleep.dynamics.cheer

The shaded greenery of Seoul's third-largest park provides a perfect habitat for fallow deer, elk, and chipmunks. The first thing you'll notice, however, is the park's resident population of city picnickers. Here, clustered in groups upon the grass or on foldable tables, families and friends chat amiably. Notice their lack of picnic hampers? Most opt to have their food arrive fresh, with local restaurants delivering treats right to the park's gates. So pack your blanket and a bottle or two, and lunch as the locals do.

NAMSAN MOUNTAIN

Map 4; 231 Samil-daero, Jung-gu; ///searches.exhaled.fancy

There are few picnic spots more romantic than N Seoul Tower, which is based at the top of Namsan Mountain. Take a steady evening stroll up the slope, admiring the swoon-worthy vistas over

If you want the views without the trek, pick up the Namsan cable car from near Myeongdong Station.

the city, before finding a choice spot among the picnicking couples at the tower's base. After all, nothing says love like *kimbap* with a view.

MONTMARTRE PARK

Map 5; Banpo-daero 37-gil, Seocho-gu; ///craters.drilled.looks

French by name, French by nature: picnic at Montmartre Park and you'll be transported to the finest Parisian *jardin*. With numerous *boulangeries*, bottle shops, and delis in the nearby French enclave of Seorae Village *(p164)*, you can stock up on cold cuts, wine, and cheese before lounging in the park. Oblige your inner Francophile, and pass a languorous afternoon over a block of Brie and a Côtes du Rhône. *Bon appétit!*

» Don't leave without spotting the lively wild rabbits that call Montmartre their home – it isn't nicknamed Rabbit Park for nothing.

BANPO HANGANG RIVER PARK

Map 5; 40 Sinbanpo-ro 11-gil, Seocho-gu; ///mime.propose.drift

Yes, this park on the bank of the Han River might be pretty, but here it's all about the picnic gear. Young Seoulites elevate the humble picnic into an art form, rocking up with a dizzying selection of kit: foldable mini tables, electric lanterns, portable fans, and luxury camping chairs. Whether you bring your own or rent equipment from the nearby picnic rental businesses, we can think of no better way to soak up those charming river views.

Solo, Pair, Crowd

No matter where you are in the city, or who you're with, there's always a sweet picnic spot offering the perfect excuse to kick back.

FLYING SOLO

Blooming lovely

One of the city's most popular green spaces, Haneul Park is adorned with a sea of colorful flowers in spring. Find a shady corner and spread out that blanket.

IN A PAIR

Railroad romance

Bring your date to Hwarangdae Railroad Park and picnic in a (slightly surreal) wonderland. Expect illuminated light gardens, funky sculptures, and a fantasy train station.

FOR A CROWD

Childish charm

Children's Grand Park is aptly named: this place is huge, and popular with kids. Bring your kids, or simply satisfy your inner child, with the park's vast selection of amusement park rides.

OLYMPIC PARK

Map 6; 424 Olympic-ro, Songpa-gu; ///saying.eyelid.copper
www.olympicpark.co.kr

The 1988 Seoul Olympics hold a special place in the heart of
Seoulites (the Games were a chance to celebrate Korea's rapid
development on a global stage, for one thing). It's only fitting, then,
that the Olympic Park is one of the city's best-loved picnic spots.
With public sports areas and a sculpture-filled art park, you won't
be stuck for things to do once you polish off your lunch.

» Don't leave without traveling on the park's Hodori Train, named
after the adorable tiger mascot of the Seoul Olympics.

SEONYUDO PARK

Map 6; 343 Seonyu-ro, Yeongdeungpo-gu; ///escapes.fade.lashed

Found on Seonyudo Island in the Han River, this park was once
a water treatment plant before it was turned into a green paradise.
The park is now connected by a footbridge to the mainland, so you
can pop for a tranquil island break in the heart of the city. And as
the lunching crowds attest, spots like this were just made for picnics.

BUKSEOUL DREAM FOREST

Map 6; Wolgye-ro, Gangbuk-gu; ///curious.jeeps.mailing

Bukseoul Dream Forest is truest to its name in the fall, when the
foliage turns the landscape into an Impressionist masterpiece
of burning red, gold, and yellow. This one's so dreamy, you'll
wish you'd packed a paintbrush with your picnic.

Heritage Sights

Despite Seoul's rush to modernize, the city proudly preserves its past. It's a living museum of timeless temples, palace grounds, and rustic hanok *villages, providing insight into the region's history.*

BUKCHON HANOK VILLAGE

Map 1; Gyedong-gil, Jongno-gu; ///showed.fetches.gently

Nothing brings Seoul's heritage to life quite like a stroll through Bukchon. Here, in the shadow of the city's soaring downtown skyscrapers, almost 900 *hanok* (traditional Korean houses) have been lovingly restored, with the grand *hanok* of Joseon-era aristocrats sitting beside humbler homes from the 1930s. Some *hanok* have even been converted into bars and galleries. A more iconic image of the city's changing face? We challenge you to find one.

NAMSANGOL HANOK VILLAGE

Map 4; 28 Toegye-ro 34-gil, Jung-gu; ///snored.womanly.gossip; www.hanokmaeul.or.kr/en

This folk village and open-air museum is a quaint love letter to Seoul's traditions, where you can don *hanbok*, learn to fold *hanji* (Korean paper), and watch flawless *tae kwon do* displays.

The highlight, though, is the five *hanok* themselves. Such is the care that has gone into preserving these striking Joseon-era houses, you'd be forgiven for thinking their 19th-century owners had simply popped out for lunch.

CHEONG WA DAE

Map 4; 1 Cheongwadae-ro, Jongno-gu; ///handy.bearings.happen;
www.reserve.opencheongwadae.kr

Named after its iconic blue-tiled roof, the Blue House served as the official home of Korea's presidents from 1948 to 2022. Since the presidential office moved to nearby Yongsan, the doors of the Blue House are now open to the public. Get up close to Seoul's political past on a guided tour of the presidential residence, before strolling the landscaped grounds (speculating, no doubt, on the diplomatic deals that went down under the garden's trees).

DEOKSUGUNG PALACE

Map 1; 99 Sejong-daero, Jung-gu; ///lifters.breeding.loosens;
www.deoksugung.go.kr

Deoksugung might be the smallest of the five palaces in Seoul, but what it lacks in size it makes up for in historical stature. It was in these hallowed halls that Emperor Gojong announced the birth of the Korean Empire in 1897, for one. Admire the architecture on a walk of the grounds, as you await the changing of the Royal Guard.

» **Don't leave without** taking a guided night tour of the palace, when the building's facade is beautifully illuminated.

DALMASA TEMPLE

Map 6; 50-26 Seodal-ro, Dongjak-gu; ///rivers.conveys.seaweed;
www.dalmasa.org

A visit to any of Seoul's Buddhist temples is sure to be special, but ask for a local's favorite, and many will point to Dalmasa. Perhaps it's the postcard-perfect location at the base of Seodal Mountain, the pink cherry blossom adorning the pathways in spring, or the welcoming monks who are happy to speak about the local flora. For those who relax in these grounds, it's all these things and more.

HEUNGINJIMUN GATE

Map 4; 288 Jong-ro, Jongno-gu; ///prevents.regime.upstairs

When Seoul's city walls were built in 1396, the eastern entrance was given an arrestingly beautiful name: *Heunginjimun*, meaning "Gate of Rising Benevolence." Now engulfed by the slightly less majestic Dongdaemun shopping district, the gate stands like a marooned time traveler, with the current stone and wood structure dating to 1869. While visiting, swing by the Seoul City Wall Museum across the road, and you'll be an authority on the city's history in no time.

CHANGDEOKGUNG PALACE

Map 4; 99 Yulgok-ro, Jongno-gu; ///lazy.lateral.month;
www.cdg.go.kr

This is the big one, the souvenir photo every tourist clamors to take. Built in 1405, Changdeokgung Palace is the best preserved of the city's royal residences, and is now a UNESCO World Heritage Site (read: forever thronged with tour groups). Look beyond the crowds, however, to experience one of the finest examples of Korea's royal architecture. Notice the harmony of the building and its grounds when preparing the perfect shot? Thank the aesthetic principles of *pungsu-jiri*, a sort of Korean feng shui.

» **Don't leave without** relaxing in the palace's not-so-secret "Secret Garden," which has hardly changed since royalty strolled here.

GILSANGSA TEMPLE
Map 4; 68 Seonjam-ro 5-gil, Seongbuk-gu; ///snored.womanly.gossip; www.kilsangsa.or.kr

There aren't many cities where you'll find a former restaurant converted into a beloved Buddhist temple, but that's what happened at Gilsangsa in 1995. The restaurant's owner, Kim Young-han, became so enamored with the writings of the monk Beopjeong that she turned her land into this oasis as a tribute to her faith. And locals are certainly glad she did, making full use of the temple's Zen Center, meditation rooms, and lush green grounds.

Try it!
TEMPLE MEALS

Gilsangsa Temple offers a donation-only food kitchen, where you can sample the humble but nourishing meals eaten by Buddhist monks. Note: the cooks will be grateful if you offer to help with the dishes.

Mountain Walks

In the Joseon era, Seoul was chosen as Korea's capital because of the eight major mountains on its border. So, go figure: peaks are big news here. Fortunately, the city's trails don't all involve strenuous climbs.

GWANAKSAN MOUNTAIN

Map 6; start at Seoul National University campus; ///survived.streaks.method

With the rare privilege of a mountain on their doorstep, it's no wonder that students at Seoul National University are such keen climbers. Take their lead and start a bracing 3-mile (5-km) hike from the west of Gwanaksan. It might not be the city's gnarliest ascent (that honor belongs to Bukhansan), but with a cliffside temple offering rad views over the city, this one's worth skipping lectures for.

INWANGSAN MOUNTAIN

Map 4; start at exit 2 of Dongnimmun Station; ///linked.mailer.behaving

The 3-mile (5-km) hike up Inwangsan has held a special place in the heart of the city for centuries. The mountain, which once marked the western edge of Seoul, is regarded as holy by local shamans. Start out from the dramatic rock formation known as Seonbawi (or

Zen Rocks) and follow the old city walls up to the peak. The route is steep, but the dreamy views over Seoul from the summit will be sure to convince you of the mountain's wonders.

» **Don't leave without** visiting Guksadang, a shamanist shrine, on the way up. It's said to house the spirit of the Joseon dynasty's founder.

ANSAN JARAK-GIL TRAIL

Map 4; start at exit 4 of Dongnimmun Station; ///frozen.cable.retiring

One for those who prefer to admire a mountain from its base, this 4-mile (7.5-km) trail follows a flat wooden deck around Ansan's forest-clad perimeter, with a patchwork of tracks leading off up the slope. The entire circular trail, which passes lush forest undergrowth, is ideal for those who prefer simple sneakers to hefty boots or have limited mobility. A mountain is more than its peak, after all.

BUKHANSAN NATIONAL PARK

Map 6; take bus 704 from Gupabal Station; ///beats.dairy.koala

Need proof that hiking is a way of life in Seoul? Just visit Bukhansan, the city's nearest national park. Come the weekend, anyone and everyone decks themselves out in their finest gear and congregates at the base of Bukhansan Mountain. While intrepid (read: foolhardy) hikers might opt for the punishingly steep Uisangneungseon course, we suggest sticking to the (slightly) gentler Bukhansanseong route. Make no mistake: this 5-mile (8-km) round trip to the peak is no casual saunter. After five hours of thigh-burning work out, you'll have earned that soju back in town.

ACHASAN MOUNTAIN

Map 6; start at exit 2 of Achasan Station; ///luggage.narrow.reinforce

The gentle slopes of Achasan in the heart of Seoul were popular before K-pop phenomenon BTS ascended the mountain on their web show back in 2018. But since then, thousands of young fans have been clamoring to follow in their footsteps. Vloggers have detailed the route they took to the peak, and the view from the summit has been streamed across endless socials. K-pop fan or not, this gentle half-a-mile (1-km) ascent is one of the city's best, offering sublime views over the Lotte Tower and other landmarks. To find the staircase at the start of the trail, follow the road around Yeonghwasa Temple; the green stairs on your right will take you up the paved paths of Achasan. Otherwise, just follow the BTS fans.

EUNGBONGSAN MOUNTAIN

Map 5; start at exit 1 of Eungbong Station; ///even.stews.patting

With its sublime views over the Han River, Eungbongsan (or "hawk peak") is where Joseon-era royals came to hunt. The prey-stalking noblemen might have gone, but nowadays the mountain has birthed a new tradition: admiring the first sunrise of the Lunar New Year. There are two main paths up to the eight-sided pagoda at the summit, each taking around an hour, with the favored 300-ft (94-m) ascent starting from Eungbong Station. Keen to watch the first new year sunrise as the locals do? This route is well lit at night, so you can safely make the climb in the small hours.

» Don't leave without trying the public exercise facilities at the summit. A work out with a view — so very Seoul.

Liked by the locals

"Hiking as we know it didn't become widely popular in Korea until the 1970s and 80s. But the mountains are entrenched in Korean lore, and mountain-going has been part of folk life here for centuries."

SHAWN MORRISSEY, FOLK HERITAGE RESEARCHER AND
TOUR GUIDE OF "DARK SIDE OF SEOUL" AND "SEOUL HIKE"

Nearby Getaways

Seoul may be the beating heart of Korea and home to half of the country's population, but beyond the city limits are idyllic natural escapes and significant historical sites, all ideal for a day trip.

GANGHWADO

1-hour 45-minute bus ride from Hapjeong Station

Korea is blessed with thousands of islands, and the fifth largest, Ganghwado, is pretty much on Seoul's doorstep. Okay, that'd make Seoul's doorstep 31 miles (50 km) long, but it's the closest island to the capital and a go-to coastal hotspot on the weekend. Feast on

fresh seafood (think salted shrimp and raw herring) in the port of Oepo, then let the ocean breeze carry you into the forested hilltops, where Korea's oldest Buddhist temple, Jeongdeung-sa, awaits.
>> Don't leave without visiting the Ganghwa Peace Observatory, from which you can peer into North Korea – Ganghwa is only separated from the DPRK by the mouth of the Han River.

SEONGMODO

50-minute train ride from Seoul Station, then 1-hour taxi from Yeongjong

Rivaling Ganghwado for a Seoulite's favorite island escape is Seongmodo – smaller, quieter, and, dare we say, dreamier. The entire island can be explored by bike in under three hours, so rent some wheels and pedal along the coastal and country roads, locking up to watch the sun set over Minmeoru Beach.

THE GARDEN OF MORNING CALM

1-hour train ride from Cheongnyangni Station, then 25-minute bus;
www.morningcalm.co.kr

Korea's nickname, "the Land of the Morning Calm," stems from the country's serene natural beauty – something that inspired both the name and landscaping of this garden. Themed sections host some 5,000 species of plant, among them gardens devoted to bonsai, conifers, and the rose of Sharon, Korea's national flower. Budding botanists would love nothing more than a weekly visit to this garden, but realistically, they save their visits for the seasonal festivals, like the winter Lighting Festival, when lights illuminate the entire garden.

EVERLAND

40-minute bus ride from Seoul Station; www.everland.com

Try finding a Korean who hasn't been to the country's largest theme park. Yes, Seoul has epic rides at Lotte World *(p143)*, but when locals really want an action-packed day, they take a trip out to Everland, where thrill-seekers of all ages are catered to. Head for heights? Make for the dramatic Rolling X-Train Coaster. Little ones in tow? Explore the adorable Magic Cookie House.

YANGSU-RI

1.5-hour subway ride from Gangbyeon Station

A bucolic little village at the periphery of Seoul's subway network, Yangsu-ri is a snapshot of rural Korea, dotted with rice fields, gentle river streams, and pine-clad mountains. It feels worlds away from the hubbub of Seoul without actually being that far, making it the perfect break on a stressful afternoon. Our advice? Leave your phone behind, disconnect, and breathe in that sweet, sweet countryside air.

THE DEMILITARIZED ZONE (DMZ)

2-hour bus ride from Dong Seoul; www.dmz.go.kr

In Seoul, the separation of the Korean Peninsula can seem a world away; a few dozen miles to the north, it's reality. The Demilitarized Zone (DMZ) is, in fact, heavily militarized, and a trip here will bring you face to face with barbed wire fences, tank traps, and a 1-mile (1.5-km) tunnel the North dug in an attempt to infiltrate the South. Most famously, though, you'll see the Joint Security Area, where

The DMZ is one of the most dangerous borders on earth, so you must join a tour to visit anywhere within it. | opposing troops stare each other down and the distance between different worlds is an invisible line. It's a sobering visit for locals, and many make the trip.

NAMI ISLAND

40-minute train ride from Hoegi Station to Gapyeong Station, then taxi to Nami Island Wharf, then ferry; www.namisum.com

You don't buy a ticket to visit Nami Island; you buy a "visa" to visit the "Nami Republic." Yes, a lot of things about this small island are a bit contrived, but it's part of its charm. Nami found fame in the early 2000s as a filming location for K-drama *Winter Sonata* – a romance that many cite as launching the Hallyu phenomenon. While the initial hordes of fans have subsided, it remains especially popular with couples, who come to stroll hand in hand along gingko-lined paths and sip iced Americanos in cute cafés.

HEYRI ART VILLAGE

1-hour bus from Hapjeong Station; www.heyri.net

If you thought Seoul's Hongdae was a creative bastion, wait until you visit Heyri Art Village. This sprawling village of contemporary galleries, artist studios, and trendy cafés was created by and for creatives of all stripes. It's the day trip budding artists and writers roll out when they need inspiration, or a like-minded community.

» Don't leave without visiting neighboring Paju Book City, home to over 200 book publishers, as well as book cafés and bookstores.

INCHEON

1-hour train ride from Seoul Station; www.incheon.go.kr

On Korea's west coast, Incheon has long served as the country's entryway, and it's where your plane will land before you take the train into Seoul. Hold off heading straight to the capital, though – there's plenty to see in this port town. So much here stands as a testament to Incheon's long history as an entrepôt, from the Chinese, Japanese, and French architecture to the Korean-Chinese black bean noodle dish, *jjajangmyeon*, invented here. Explore the city's Chinatown on one side of Incheon Station, then check out Wolmido Island's amusement park rides and sashimi restaurants on the other. It'll be a day well spent before traveling to Seoul.

» **Don't leave without** visiting Incheon's Songdo development – a new, futuristic city built from scratch on reclaimed land. It's what Korea wants its future to look like.

HWASEONG

40-minute bus ride from Sadang Station; www.swcf.or.kr

Traditional Korean culture values filial piety, so by any measure King Jeongjo would have to be named World's Best Son. To house the tomb of his father, he built this magnificent fortress. Completed in 1796, this was the era's most stunning technological achievement, its cutting-edge design home to the country's largest gate and nearly 4 miles (6.5 km) of walls. Impressively, this was all built in under three years. It was intended to be the hub of a new Korean capital, but we all know what part of the country got that title. Still, those with an eye for architecture and a love for history visit the fortress to think about what could've been, exploring the watchtowers, command pavilions, and secret gates that troops once used to attack the enemy. As tributes to fathers go, this one takes some beating.

KOREAN FOLK VILLAGE

1-hour bus from Gangnam Station; www.koreanfolk.co.kr

You might be tempted to dismiss this recreation of a Joseon-era village as a tourist trap, but you'd be wrong to do so. Korea's folk villages offer a distilled version of country life, and exist somewhere between an open-air museum (for tourists, yes) and a genuine repository of rapidly fading customs. The Korean Folk Village is one of the most expertly done – a snapshot of Joseon-era living where artisans make straw shoes and traditional musicians perform in front of tile-roofed houses. On traditional holidays, the village celebrates just as Koreans did in centuries past, playing folk music on Lunar New Year and making red-bean porridge on the Lunar winter solstice. It's a soothing reminder of what life was like before all those smartphones and robots took over.

Try it!
GET CRAFTY

Live like a Joseon-era artisan at the Korean Folk Village with a traditional dyeing workshop, where you'll use natural materials like sappan wood to add subtle color to a handkerchief. Check the website for times.

A day strolling the
Seoul city wall

The building of Seoul's fortress wall started back in 1396, with periods of construction and refurb continuing until 1869. Much of it remains intact today, and while hiking its full 11.5 miles (18.5 km) is a great way to see the city, it's a lot to tackle at once. This four-hour route (not including stops) follows two of its prettiest, and, in our humble opinion, most interesting sections, passing historic sites, mountain peaks, and quaint villages.

1. Changuimun Gate
118 Changuimun-ro,
Jongno-gu
///tell.symphony.jetted

**2. Malbawi
Information Center**
40 Samcheong-ro 11-gil,
Seongbuk-gu
///below.return.fortress

3. Bukjeong Village
///walking.photo.oval

4. Naksan Park
41 Naksan-gil, Jongno-gu;
www.parks.seoul.go.kr
///riots.bumpy.bangle

5. Ihwa Mural Village
///dangerously.embodied.
sliders

6. Seoul City Wall Museum
283 Yulgok-ro, Jongno-gu;
www.museum.seoul.go.kr/
scwm/NR_index.do
///stuff.contacts.taker

📍 **January 21
Incident Pine Tree**
///eyelash.repair.missions

📍 **Sukjeongmun**
///teamed.upon.brightly

BUAM-
DONG

**Set off from
CHANGUIMUN GATE**

In the Joseon era, this gate controlled entry to the capital from the northwest. The current 1742 reconstruction is the only one of the wall's four minor gates to remain intact. today.

INWANGSAN-RO

SAJIK
DON

SEODAEMUN-
GU

CHUNGHYEON-
DONG

MAPO-DAERO

Bullet holes on the **January 21 Incident Pine Tree** *mark North Korea's attempt to assassinate the South's president in 1968.*

NAEBUSUNHWAN-RO

SEONGBUK-GU

DONAM-DONG

DONGSOMUN-RO

Gaze out from MALBAWI INFORMATION CENTER
Take a breather and scope out Seoul from two viewpoints, one that looks west across the Seongbuk area and one that looks south over palaces.

2

3

The north represents negative energy in traditional philosophy, so **Sukjeongmun**, *the city's main northern gate, was rarely opened.*

Amble through BUKJEONG VILLAGE
This cluster of homes is a "moon village": a settlement that sprang up on hillsides in the postwar years. The area often serves as a filming spot for period K-dramas.

Chill out in NAKSAN PARK
Pass Hyehwamun Gate en route to this lovely green space, where cherry trees bloom in the spring and sprawling vistas await year-round.

4

SAMCHEONG-DONG

JONGNO-GU

JOGNO-DONG

JONG-RO

SAMIL-DAERO

Explore the alleys of IHWA MURAL VILLAGE
Admire the murals lining this area, then pop into a café for a snack. Remember, people live here, so be mindful when photographing the street art.

5

6 ### End at the SEOUL CITY WALL MUSEUM
Learn about the history of this impressive fortification, then make plans to tackle another section, perhaps.

SEOUL PLAZA

SEJONG-DAERO

JUNG-GU

TOEGYE-RO

0 kilometers   1
0 miles   1

With a little research and preparation, this city will feel like a home away from home. Check out these websites to ensure a healthy, safe stay in Seoul.

Seoul
DIRECTORY

SAFE SPACES

Seoul is generally a friendly, welcoming city, but should you feel uneasy or need to find your community, there are spaces and resources to turn to.

www.enghotline.cafe24.com
Women's organization offering counseling and emergency shelter.

www.help0365.or.kr
Crisis center providing counseling and legal assistance for women who have experienced sexual or violent abuse.

www.koreaislam.org
Seoul's largest mosque and Muslim community center.

www.lgbtpride.or.kr
Multilingual legal consultation services for the LGBTQ+ community.

www.rainbowfoundation.co.kr
Foundation providing counseling services for LGBTQ+ people and allies.

HEALTH

Health care in Korea isn't free, so it's important to take out comprehensive health insurance for your visit. If you do need medical assistance, there are many affordable hospitals, walk-in clinics, and pharmacies with English-speaking doctors across Seoul.

www.120dasan.or.kr
Hotline and online portal offering assistance with travel-related difficulties, including making medical appointments.

www.e-gen.or.kr
Directory of pharmacies, emergency rooms, and other medical services based on user location.

www.khap.org
Sexual health support center that offers free STI testing.

www.medical.visitseoul.net
English-language directory of hospitals.

www.pharm114.or.kr
Directory of 24-hour pharmacies.

www.snuh.org
One of Seoul's central hospitals, with English-speaking doctors and dentists.

TRAVEL SAFETY ADVICE
Before you travel – and while you're here – always keep tabs on Seoul's latest regulations and security measures.

www.eng.safekorea.go.kr
National Disaster and Safety Portal providing live updates on natural disasters and emergencies, as well as a directory of nearby shelters.

www.english.seoul.go.kr
The Seoul Metropolitan Government's online portal offers the latest information on security, health, and local regulations.

www.lost112.go.kr
Lost-and-found service operated by the police.

www.police.go.kr
Korean National Police Agency website with a directory for tourist-specific police services.

ACCESSIBILITY
Transportation services, hotels, and museums have improved enormously when it comes to accessibility, with audio and visual information systems, elevators, and accessible turnstiles. That said, Seoul's uneven pavements can prove tricky for wheelchair users or those with reduced mobility. These resources make exploring the city easier.

www.access.visitkorea.or.kr
Searchable directory of accessible restaurants, travel destinations, and lodging across Korea.

www.moyeoyou.kr
Directory providing country-wide information on accessible restaurants, destinations, hotels, and attractions in Korea.

www.seouldanurim.net
Seoul Tourism Organization's specialty accessible tourism center, offering a range of resources including recommendations, transportation assistance, and organized tours.

INDEX

ACKNOWLEDGMENTS

Meet the illustrator

Award-winning British illustrator David Doran is based in a studio by the sea in Falmouth, Cornwall. When not drawing and designing, David tries to make the most of the beautiful area in which he's based; sea-swimming all year round, running the coastal paths, and generally spending as much time outside as possible.

Main Contributors Beth Eunhee Hong, Arian Khameneh, Allison Needels, Charles Usher

Senior Editor Zoë Rutland

Editors Alex Pathe, Danielle Watt

Designers Jordan Lambley, Divyanshi Shreyaskar

Proofreader Stephanie Smith

Indexer Helen Peters

Senior Cartographic Editor Casper Morris

Cartography Manager Suresh Kumar

Cartographer Ashif

Jacket Designers Jordan Lambley, Sarah Snelling

Jacket Illustrator David Doran

Senior Production Editor Jason Little

Senior Production Controller Samantha Cross

Managing Editor Hollie Teague

Managing Art Editor Sarah Snelling

Art Director Maxine Pedliham

Publishing Director Georgina Dee

First edition 2023

Published in Great Britain by Dorling Kindersley Limited, DK, One Embassy Gardens, 8 Viaduct Gardens, London SW11 7BW, UK

The authorised representative in the EEA is Dorling Kindersley Verlag GmbH. Arnulfstr. 124, 80636 Munich, Germany

Published in the United States by DK Publishing, 1745 Broadway, 20th Floor, New York, NY 10019, USA

Copyright © 2023 Dorling Kindersley Limited
A Penguin Random House Company
23 24 25 26 10 9 8 7 6 5 4 3 2 1

A CIP catalog record for this book is available from the British Library.
A catalog record for this book is available from the Library of Congress.
ISSN: 1542 1554
ISBN: 978 0 2416 3304 5
Printed and bound in China.
www.dk.com

A NOTE FROM DK EYEWITNESS

The world is fast-changing and it's keeping us folk at DK Eyewitness on our toes. We've worked hard to ensure that this edition of Seoul Like a Local is up-to-date and reflects today's favourite places but we know that standards shift, venues close and new ones pop up in their place. So, if you notice something has closed, we've got something wrong or left something out, we want to hear about it. Please drop us a line at travelguides@dk.com